REGINA MOURADIAN

THE HERMITAGE EFFECT

How Bill Browder Went from Ally to Enemy of Russia

outskirts
press

The Hermitage Effect
How Bill Browder Went from Ally to Enemy of Russia
All Rights Reserved.
Copyright © 2020 Regina Mouradian
v2.0

The opinions expressed in this manuscript are solely the opinions of the author and do not represent the opinions or thoughts of the publisher. The author has represented and warranted full ownership and/or legal right to publish all the materials in this book.

This book may not be reproduced, transmitted, or stored in whole or in part by any means, including graphic, electronic, or mechanical without the express written consent of the publisher except in the case of brief quotations embodied in critical articles and reviews.

Outskirts Press, Inc.
http://www.outskirtspress.com

ISBN: 978-1-9772-2419-4

Cover Photo © 2020 www.gettyimages.com. All rights reserved - used with permission.

Outskirts Press and the "OP" logo are trademarks belonging to Outskirts Press, Inc.

PRINTED IN THE UNITED STATES OF AMERICA

Introduction

This book reviews the circumstances surrounding the death of a Russian tax accountant, Sergei Magnitsky. It will then examine the subsequent media manipulation by Hedge Fund manager, Bill Browder, who dominates the narrative. This book will also examine if Sergei Magnitsky was a whistleblower in the theft of two hundred and thirty million dollars from the Russian Treasury.

Table of Contents

Chapter 1 1
   A music publicist, a Russian lawyer,
   and the son of a billionaire walk into a Tower

Chapter 2 29
   The Browder Family and Stalin.

Chapter 3 36
   Who is Bill Browder?

Chapter 4 39
   Browder goes to Moscow

Chapter 5 52
   Renaissance vs Hermitage

Chapter 6 59
   Browder gets kicked out of Russia

Chapter 7 66
   Framing Russian Cops

Chapter 8 78
   Magnitsky's year in jail and death

Chapter 9 95
   Magnitsky is dead. The Magnitsky Project is Born

Chapter 10 107
   Are Veselnitskaya and Rimma the real whistleblowers?

Chapter 11 111
    Is Magnitsky a whistleblower?
Chapter 12 121
    Where did the money go?
Chapter 13 127
    Browder, Veselnitskaya, and The Daily Show
Chapter 14 132
    How did we get here?
Chapter 15 136
    Is Perepilichny a whistleblower?
Chapter 16 144
    Magnitsky's Legacy

Epilogue 153
Bibliography 155
Notes 164
Index 173

Chapter 1

A MUSIC PUBLICIST, A RUSSIAN LAWYER, AND THE SON OF A BILLIONAIRE WALK INTO A TOWER

How should I set the scene for this book?

It was a dark cold wintry night in New York City and I was running for my life. The beads of sweat trickled down my face as I fled my nemesis with every ounce of strength I had. My chest was getting tighter as I gulped in the sharp freezing air resisting looking back to check the distance between us. I could hear the shouts of the KGB agent getting louder and closer. Just don't slip on the ice Bill, and you might be able to escape. If I was twenty years younger I could outrun him, but my fifty year old legs betrayed me. I felt his firm grip grab me by the shoulders and he forced me to turn around and look him in the eyes. His beady eyes stared menacingly into mine. The visible air we exhaled mixing together as we both panted heavily from the chase. "You've been served," he grunted, and I dropped my head defeated.

There was nothing left I could do. I traipsed in my new Berluti Scritto shoes through the New York City slush, back to my heated limo. Drive! I said to my driver. And he drove.

This sounds like a novel but it's all true! This is how financier, Bill Browder, might set up the scene in his book, but I don't need to describe this scene. It was caught on video and you can Google it yourself and watch on YouTube. See, video kind of ruins the moment when you can't manipulate what happened and eyewitnesses can contradict your fable. That's the intent of this book, to crack the veneer of a packaged book, *Red Notice*, written by Bill Browder. I won't describe Russians how Bill does. Here is a quote from his recent discussion at the University of Chicago. "Bad guys in the Putin regime have all come from a terrible environment from the moment they emerge into the world. It was horribleness and treachery and hardship and, just, you know, nothing good has ever happened to them." So, if you want descriptions of citizens of Russia like that, go read *Red Notice*. If you want to just hear facts, then welcome. Oh! By the way, that chase in New York City? Turns out it wasn't KGB, just an American serving him a subpoena to testify in the New York courts.

So, let's start over...

This is a story about mystery and murder. It's a story about several murders, or, maybe no murders at all. Was Sergei Magnitsky murdered? Bill Browder says he was beaten to death with rubber batons by eight prison guards for one hour and eighteen minutes. The Russian Federation says Browder was complicit in the murder of Sergei Magnitsky by poison. There are dozens of accusations flying around this new Cold War between Bill Browder, who, you could say, is a representative of "The West" vs "The Russian Federation" and Putin's government. So far Browder has accused The Russian Federation of the murders of Sergei Magnitsky, Alexander Perepilichny, Octai Gasanov, Valery Kurochkin, and Sergei Korobeinikov. Russia has responded with accusing Browder of being involved in the planning of these same, allegedly murdered people. Browder has also insinuated that the Russian Federation is behind the deaths of other Russians, including the playwrights who wrote the play *One Hour Eighteen Minutes*, a play about the investigation into Magnitsky's death. Elena Gremina and her husband, Mikhail Ugarov, both died of heart attacks. Browder tweets out that the playwrights, Mr Ugarov and Ms Gremina's causes of death were 'heart attacks' in quotation marks, implying malfeasance. Browder has also hinted the fatal helicopter crash of a General Prosecutor in Russia was sinister because he was "connected" to Nataliya Veselnitskaya. Saak Karapetyan's helicopter crash couldn't be just an accident if Browder can spin murder into the story without any evidence. Even a Russian journalist, Sergey Dorenko, who crashed his motorcycle, in what Browder describes as a 'freak accident' doesn't escape suspicion. When no one else is bringing up his death as suspicious, Browder will add his two cents of murder. I contacted an associate of Ms Gremina's, a translator of her play from Russian to English, who was surprised when I told him Browder was spreading the rumor there was something sinister in Elena Gremina's death. He knew of no one in her inner circle whispering murder. She was in poor health for most of the year before she suffered a fatal heart attack.

It's reckless remarks of murder by Browder that feeds my skepticism of any narrative he tries to put forth. What about Ms Gremina's family? Is it fair to them to have rumors swirling around she was murdered? When Browder brazenly stated Alexander Perepilichny was poisoned, his wife had to wait years for his life insurance payment. Finally, the UK Surrey police, the coroners, and the courts stated he died of natural causes. Did Browder show any empathy towards Perepilichny's widow? Some would say Browder is a provocateur, who will take the opportunity of any death of a critic of Putin and turn it into a far more murky and nefarious explanation to score points for his "Putin is bad" team. Others think Browder is a champion of human rights, calling out injustice wherever he sees it. They believe Russian citizens look to him for inspiration for potential in their country. To be free after the authoritarian government of Putin is toppled. Any event that places Russia in a bad light is highlighted by Browder, even before the event is over and details have not yet emerged. If a protestor is hit with a rubber baton by the Russian police at a protest, say, a protest organized by activist Alexey Navalny, Browder runs to Twitter demanding the name of the Russian cop be put on his Magnitsky Act list for sanctions. If a Russian man is arrested "just because he tweeted", Browder cries horrible oppression. He fails to mention the tweet was a specific threat to a specific cop about killing the cop's child. This back and forth doesn't make the headlines like say, "Trump vs Pelosi" epic battles, but it is similar in nature in that he is trying to control the narrative and frame an event in the context that makes Browder the "good guy" and Putin always and forever the "bad guy".

The extremes of Browder's character with his United States image vs his Russia image could not be further opposite on a spectrum. Browder is portrayed as a hero on Western TV, and a villain on Russian TV. Perhaps he is neither but is nothing more than a liar and a manipulator of circumstances that have now spun out of his control. To continue the lies, he creates more and more smearing of more and more truth seekers. He has become the character in the Matt Damon film, *'The Talented Mr. Ripley'*, falling further down the rabbit hole of his own making, too deep now to crawl back out. I think trying to search for the truth in this story is important though. Why is it important to me? I haven't quite figured that out yet, but it is definitely a murder mystery I want to solve.

My journey on the path of researching Bill Browder began when I watched his Senate testimony in July 27th, 2017. The topic was circumstances surrounding the infamous "Trump Tower meeting" during the height of the 2016 Presidential campaign. This was when Donald J. Trump had just clinched the Republican primary and was full speed ahead in his battle to win the Presidency. Like many Americans, I was very curious about the circumstances around the 2016 election with all the unusual leaks that occurred. The dumping of DNC emails through Wikileaks right before the Democratic convention was a big event, resulting in the firing of the DNC chairman, Debbie Wasserman Schultz.

Browder was testifying before the Senate Judiciary Committee on July 27th, 2017, about his experiences with Russian operatives and how he believed the Russian government was behind setting up the meeting Nataliya Veselnitskaya attended at Trump Tower. Ms. Veselnitskaya, a Russian lawyer, was in town to represent her client in the *Prevezon vs US* case in the SDNY (Southern District of New York). Those listening to her story on the receiving end at Trump Tower were Donald Trump Jr, Paul Manafort, and Jared Kushner. Rob Goldstone, a music publicist, set up the meeting sending emails back and forth to Trump Jr. Also attending were the following people; Anatoli Samachornov, Ms Veselnitskaya's translator; Rinat Akhmetshin, a former Soviet intelligence officer and now American lobbyist; and Irakly "Ike" Kaveladze, Vice President of the Agalarov family's real estate company. Ike represented the Agalarov family at the meeting, So, in total there were eight people at the meeting, and all have given sworn testimony to the Senate Judiciary committee of their involvement. Ms Veselnitskaya is a Russian lawyer who was in town to represent her client, Denis Katsyv, in the New York courts. Ms Veselnitskaya submitted a lengthy testimony to Senator Grassley's Committee. "Ike" Kaveladze gave his testimony because he represented the Agalarov family for the meeting. Aras Agalarov is a real estate developer and businessman in Russia, and his son, Emin Agalarov, is a pop star who is represented by music publicist, Rob Goldstone. The Agalarov family knows the Trump family through the entertainment industry and real estate. Donald Trump, Goldstone, and Emin all attended the 2013 *Miss Universe Pageant* in Moscow. Aras Agalarov organized the pageant and was pitching ideas of a Trump Tower in Moscow during the trip. The Agalarov family also have close connections to the country of Azerbaijan since Emin's ex wife's father was the President of the country.

It was probably in the Fall of 2017 that I watched Bill Browder's Senate testimony on one of my many nights going down the rabbit hole of YouTube videos that were recommended once you finished a previous video on a related topic. I had never heard of the man, but as I watched his testimony my gut instinct was I thought he wasn't being truthful. Again, this was only a first impression and I was only going on a visceral response. When I looked at the comments under the video, I saw a lot of people were critical of his character and I read some of the opinions without putting too much weight behind them. Like many comments on YouTube, they turn negative quickly no matter who the subject matter is highlighting.

Jump ahead a month or so and I had joined Twitter to further my curiosity about the 2016 Presidential campaign. One of the first interactions I had was with a Corbyn supporter in the U.K, "Mickey". He posted a Tweet about a documentary called "*The Magnitsky Act*", about Bill Browder and Sergei Magnitsky. I read a description about the Producer and the Director of the film and it seemed to be the same documentary that Browder was referring to in his 2017 Senate testimony. He was talking about Russian disinformation making its way to the halls of Congress, and FARA violations to those promoting the film and trying to repeal the Magnitsky Act. I realized this documentary was the one that was played at the Newseum on June 13th, 2016, and the screening was funded by some of the people that attended the "Trump Tower meeting", so this piqued my curiosity. I know many of those that attended the Trump Tower meeting also attended the screening of the documentary and were being scrutinized for their roles and motives in attending.

In his July 2017 Senate testimony, Browder described how this group; Rinat Akhmetshin, Nataliya Veselnitskaya, and others, started an NGO called HRAGI (they registered February 18, 2016, in Delaware). Its purpose was to repeal the Magnitsky Act and restore Russian adoptions. Rinat Akhmetshin, a former Soviet intelligence officer naturalized as an American citizen was a lobbyist in DC, who was also summoned in front of the Senate Judiciary Committee in July 2017, to explain the origins of his lobbying money.

Browder can spin a good story and in an hour of testimony critiquing this lobbying group, he performed an effective character assassination on the bunch with all the Senators nodding their heads solemnly throughout his testimony. Browder begins by explaining how he contacted Senator Ben Cardin and Senator John McCain in 2010 in attempts to get justice for his murdered Russian lawyer outside of Russia, as the Russian government were covering up Sergei Magnitsky's murder. No one seems to care Bill Browder, a UK citizen, didn't file for a FARA in his lobbying efforts, but I digress. In 2012 The Magnitsky Act was passed in the US House of Representatives 364 to 43 and later in the Senate 92 to 4. On December 14, 2012, President Obama signed the Sergei Magnitsky Act into Law.

The Magnitsky Act is a law formally known as the Jackson-Vanik Act that punishes those in Russia who commit human rights abuses. Now with The Global Magnitsky Act passed, other countries human rights abusers can be added to the list as well. Browder argues targeted personal sanctions are more effective because they can act as a deterrent to those crooks who bank in the West. They may think twice about their actions, knowing they could be denied banking and entry into countries that abide by The Magnitsky Act.

Proposals to take Sergei Magnitsky's name off the Global Magnitsky Act were unsuccessful. Browder's lobbying efforts for both 2012 Magnitsky Act, and later, The Global Magnitsky Act, were successful and the laws easily passed with bipartisan support. Both laws have strengthened the US treasury's power to freeze the assets of human rights abusers from Russia and any other country. After these acts were passed in America, Browder continued testimonies in front of other countries parliaments, retelling the same fifteen minute story of his murdered lawyer, Sergei Magnitsky. In campaigning all over the world, countries such as UK, Canada, Estonia, Latvia, and Lithuania have now passed their own version of The Magnitsky Act that freezes the assets of human rights abusers from any country. Presently there are dozens of Russians on each of these countries lists and these Russian citizens, although free to spend and travel outside of areas that are not on the list, are unable to travel or spend their money in the countries where their visas are banned. Their bank accounts are frozen and are denied opening accounts in the future.

Browder is actively trying to get a European Union Magnitsky Act passed, as this is more of a punishment to Russians who travel and bank more in Europe than The United States. A European Parliament Magnitsky list has been released, but it is largely symbolic as it has no authority over any treasury, banking systems, or visa approvals. The European Commission has more power and Browder is also lobbying this executive body. As Browder stated in his US Senate testimony, "I hope my story will help you understand the methods of Russian operatives in Washington and how they use U.S enablers to achieve foreign policy goals without disclosing those interests."

So, with reading a little bit of the background on financier Bill Browder, I decided I wanted to watch this documentary about The Magnitsky Act. It was more difficult to obtain than just clicking on the link to Netflix. The documentary was effectively blacklisted by many websites after its viewing at the Newseum. I had to contact the Norwegian Producer of the film, Torstein Grude, on Twitter. He asked for my email to send me a password to unlock the movie from a website so I could watch for free. I was very hesitant to communicate with him through these channels. I would no longer be anonymous, and the whole interaction seemed sketchy. I waited a day or so and did not tell my husband about my communication. I felt like I was wiring my bank account to a Nigerian Prince and if I was swindled, I didn't want my husband to say "I told you so" when it turned negative. So, with trepidation I punched in the code and the documentary began on my iPhone with my headphones on, to not disturb my husband sleeping.

The documentary was excellent and reinforced my skepticism I had for Bill Browder's character that is never challenged on news channels like Fox and CNN. When faced with a sincere question from the Director, Browder appeared flustered and not able to sort out contradictions in his version of the story versus what open sources showed Nekrasov. The Director of The Magnitsky Act documentary is a Russian by the name of Andrei Nekrasov. He has directed other films focused on Russia, including a documentary about the Chechen War and another about the poisoning of Litvinenko called *"Rebellion: the Litvinenko Case"*. His twitter handle is @antiputinismus, so it appears he is a critic of Russian President Vladimir Putin. Nekrasov was initially welcomed by Bill Browder to tell his, and Magnitsky's story. At the beginning of the documentary you see Browder and Nekrasov interacting at dinner and in Browder's office discussing the layout of the film. Browder is looking over sketches of the Russian police raiding Browder's Hedge Fund company, Hermitage Capital Management. They are confiscating documents relating to a corruption case. Browder says the sketches of the Russian police with drawn rifles and masks was a bit dramatic, but he seemed to approve the over dramatization of the raid. The first half of the documentary goes along with Browder's narrative of how events transpired, but as the film goes on, it's more about the director having doubts about Browder's story. Nekrasov is conflicted in completing the documentary following Browder's version, or following a different path of facts based on interviews and documents he discovers along the way. I felt a connection with Andrei Nekrasov in his struggle to tell the story about Sergei Magnitsky. He wanted to show respect to the deceased, possibly murdered Russian citizen, but is conflicted with open sources that contradict Bill Browder's version of events.

After watching this film, I was even more curious about what the truth was surrounding the death of Sergei Magnitsky. Where did the truth lie? Most likely somewhere in the middle of the Russian Federation's version and Bill Browder's version, but how close to the middle? Where on the spectrum did the truth fall? Maybe there are many spectrums for each chapter of this story. One lie by each side does not negate their position, but just opens a seed of doubt. I have caught both sides in lies, but whose lies are bigger and more important? What does the bigger picture entail? So what if Browder may have used the convenient death of a witness to his crimes in Russia to avoid prosecution for his tax evasion in the country? Isn't that minor compared to the five murder charges the Russian Federation is willing to charge Bill Browder with if Russia is ever successful in their attempts to have him extradited? Would I cheer his extradition to serve his convictions in Russia? The convictions determined in absentia?

These are questions I struggle with when I'm in the weeds researching this story and come up for air to look at the bigger picture of what are the repercussions for believing one narrative over the other. If Browder is lying about his experiences, does that minimize others who have been victims of human rights abuse in Russia? Is the Russian prison system an outlier in its cruelty compared to the US prison system? Would Russia be justified, in say, sanctioning Sheriff Arpaio or other US government employees for criticisms of their alleged abuse of human rights?

Browder is always stating that Putin was furious with the sanctions placed on those involved in the Magnitsky case and Putin's response was to ban adoption of Russian children to Americans. This isn't entirely accurate. Russia had long before Magnitsky died been discussing options to curb adoptions after the unfortunate death of an adopted

Russian child that was left in the hot car when his dad forgot to drop him off at daycare. The story made world news and Russia passed a law named after the young child who died called the Dima Yakovlev Law. Putin signed the law on December 28th, 2012, and it took effect January 1st, 2013. The Dima Yakovlev Law passed two weeks after the Magnitsky Act, but it was debated in the Russian parliament, the Duma, well before it was signed into law. To say it was a direct parallel escalation tactic in response to the Magnitsky Act is too simple an analogy to address the years Russian politicians like Ekaterina Lakhova, campaigned for sanctions on the poor American individual who was found responsible for the child's death. Why are Preet Bharara and Michael McFaul put on the Dima Yakovlev sanctions list even though they were nowhere near Dima that tragic day? We will get to that.

Critics of the Magnitsky Act argue that Sergei Magnitsky died of neglect, similar to circumstances surrounding Dima Yakovlev' unfortunate death. Both The Dima Yakovlev Act and The Sergei Magnitsky Act can be used as political weapons for countries to sanction individuals without due process. For instance, a police officer by the name of Pavel Karpov is sanctioned by the Magnitsky Act and banned from the US, but there is nowhere for him to take his case to if he wanted due process, such as the right to face his accusers or a right to a jury of his peers. There is no chance to present his side of the story and no opportunity to defend himself against the charges outlined by our US Treasury. In essence, once the US treasury puts an individual on the sanctions list, there is very little that individual can do to take themselves off the list. If Browder was falsely accusing Pavel Karpov of being complicit in the death of Sergei Magnitsky, Karpov has no right to appeal this decision.

Same goes for Americans that were banned from Russia with the passing of The Dima Yakovlev Act that had nothing to do with adoptions. People sanctioned by Russia like former US Ambassador to Russia, Michael McFaul, or Department of Homeland Security Agent

Todd Hyman, have no opportunity to appeal their ban or argue their case in Russia or International Courts.

These were some of the dilemmas Andrei Nekrasov agonized over when attempting to tell the story accurately in his documentary, *The Magnitsky Act*. The transition from the beginning of the film where he is telling the story verbatim from Browder's viewpoint, to the end when he discovers the many contradictions in the story, is a transformation of a man struggling to find the truth. I find Nekrasov a sympathetic character and understand his frustration trying to wrap his brain around the story.

At the beginning of *The Magnitsky Act* documentary, Browder is interviewed, and Browder tells his story brilliantly. It is an emotionally compelling story, and you are quickly sympathetic to Sergei Magnitsky and Bill Browder. Browder has told the story so many times, and this excerpt taken from his Senate Judiciary testimony helps to explain his version as he told it to Andrei Nekrasov. Part of Browder's testimony was printed in *The Atlantic* by journalist, Rosie Grey. **"I am the founder and CEO of Hermitage Capital Management. I grew up in Chicago, but for the last 28 years I've lived in Moscow and London, and am now a British citizen. From 1996 to 2005, my firm, Hermitage Capital, was one of the largest investment advisers in Russia with more than $4 billion invested in Russian stocks.**

Russia has a well-known reputation for corruption; unfortunately, I discovered that it was far worse than many had thought. While working in Moscow I learned that Russian oligarchs stole from shareholders, which included the fund I advised. Consequently, I had an interest in fighting this endemic corruption, so my firm started doing detailed research on exactly how the oligarchs stole the vast amounts of money that they did. When we were finished with our research we would share it with the domestic and international media.

For a time, this naming and shaming campaign worked remarkably well and led to less corruption and increased share prices in the companies we invested in. Why? Because President Vladimir Putin and I shared the same set of enemies. When Putin was first elected in 2000, he found that the oligarchs had misappropriated much of the president's power as well. They stole power from him while stealing money from my investors. In Russia, your enemy's enemy is your friend, and even though I've never met Putin, he would often step into my battles with the oligarchs and crack down on them.

The results of this change came very quickly. On November 13, 2005, as I was flying into Moscow from a weekend away, I was stopped at Sheremetyevo airport, detained for 15 hours, deported, and declared a threat to national security.

Eighteen months after my expulsion a pair of simultaneous raids took place in Moscow. Over 25 Interior Ministry officials barged into my Moscow office and the office of the American law firm that represented me. The officials seized all the corporate documents connected to the investment holding companies of the funds that I advised. I didn't know the purpose of these raids so I hired the smartest Russian lawyer I knew, a 35-year-old named Sergei Magnitsky. I asked Sergei to investigate the purpose of the raids and try to stop whatever illegal plans these officials had.

Sergei went out and investigated. He came back with the most astounding conclusion of corporate identity theft: The documents seized by the Interior Ministry were used to fraudulently re-register our Russian investment holding companies to a man named Viktor Markelov, a known criminal convicted of manslaughter. After more digging, Sergei discovered that the stolen companies were used by the perpetrators to misappropriate $230 million of taxes that our companies had paid to the Russian government in the previous year.

I had always thought Putin was a nationalist. It seemed inconceivable that he would approve of his officials stealing $230 million from the Russian state. Sergei and I were sure that this was a rogue operation and if we just brought it to the attention of the Russian authorities, the "good guys" would get the "bad guys" and that would be the end of the story.

We filed criminal complaints with every law enforcement agency in Russia, and Sergei gave sworn testimony to the Russian State Investigative Committee (Russia's FBI) about the involvement of officials in this crime.

However, instead of arresting the people who committed the crime, Sergei was arrested. Who took him? The same officials he had testified against. On November 24, 2008, they came to his home, handcuffed him in front of his family, and threw him into pre-trial detention.

Sergei's captors immediately started putting pressure on him to withdraw his testimony. They put him in cells with 14 inmates and eight beds, leaving the lights on 24 hours a day to impose sleep deprivation. They put him in cells with no heat and no windowpanes, and he nearly froze to death. They put him in cells with no toilet, just a hole in the floor and sewage bubbling up. They moved him from cell to cell in the middle of the night without any warning. During his 358 days in detention he was forcibly moved multiple times.

They did all of this because they wanted him to withdraw his testimony against the corrupt Interior Ministry officials, and to sign a false statement that he was the one who stole the $230 million—and that he had done so on my instruction.

Sergei refused. In spite of the grave pain they inflicted upon him, he would not perjure himself or bear false witness.

After six months of this mistreatment, Sergei's health seriously deteriorated. He developed severe abdominal pains, he lost 40 pounds, and he was diagnosed with pancreatitis and gallstones and prescribed an operation for August 2009. However, the operation never occurred. A week before he was due to have surgery, he was moved to a maximum security prison called Butyrka, which is considered to be one of the harshest prisons in Russia. Most significantly for Sergei, there were no medical facilities there to treat his medical conditions.

At Butyrka, his health completely broke down. He was in agonizing pain. He and his lawyers wrote 20 desperate requests for medical attention, filing them with every branch of the Russian criminal justice system. All of those requests were either ignored or explicitly denied in writing.

After more than three months of untreated pancreatitis and gallstones, Sergei Magnitsky went into critical condition. The Butyrka authorities did not want to have responsibility for him, so they put him in an ambulance and sent him to another prison that had medical facilities. But when he arrived there, instead of putting him in the emergency room, they put him in an isolation cell, chained him to a bed, and eight riot guards came in and beat him with rubber batons.

That night he was found dead on the cell floor.

Sergei Magnitsky died on November 16, 2009, at the age of 37, leaving a wife and two children.

I received the news of his death early the next morning. It was by far the most shocking, heart-breaking, and life-changing news I've ever received.

Sergei Magnitsky was murdered as my proxy. If Sergei had not been my lawyer, he would still be alive today.

That morning I made a vow to Sergei's memory, to his family, and to myself that I would seek justice and create consequences for the people who murdered him. For the last seven and a half years, I've devoted my life to this cause.

Even though this case was characterized by injustice all the way through, the circumstances of Sergei's torture and death were so extreme that I was sure some people would be prosecuted. Unlike other deaths in Russian prisons, which are largely undocumented, Sergei had written everything down. In his 358 days in detention, Sergei wrote over 400 complaints detailing his abuse. In those complaints he described who did what to him, as well as where, how, when, and why. He was able to pass his hand-written complaints to his lawyers, who dutifully filed them with the Russian authorities. Although his complaints were either ignored or rejected, copies of them were retained. As a result, we have the most well-documented case of human rights abuse coming out of Russia in the last 35 years.

When I began the campaign for justice with this evidence, I thought that the Russian authorities would have no choice but to prosecute at least some of the officials involved in Sergei Magnitsky's torture and murder. It turns out I could not have been more wrong. Instead of prosecuting, the Russian authorities circled the wagons and exonerated everybody involved. They even went so far as to offer promotions and state honors to those most complicit in Sergei's persecution.

It became obvious that if I was going to get any justice for Sergei Magnitsky, I was going to have to find it outside of Russia.

But how does one get justice in the West for a murder that took place in Russia? Criminal justice is based on jurisdiction: One cannot prosecute someone in New York for a murder committed in Moscow. As I thought about it, the murder of Sergei Magnitsky was done to cover up the theft of $230 million from the Russian Treasury. I knew that the people who stole that money wouldn't keep it in Russia. As easily as they stole the money, it could be stolen from them. These people keep their ill-gotten gains in the West, where property rights and rule of law exist. This led to the idea of freezing their assets and banning their visas here in the West. It would not be true justice but it would be much better than the total impunity they enjoyed.

In 2010, I traveled to Washington and told Sergei Magnitsky's story to Senators Benjamin Cardin and John McCain. They were both shocked and appalled and proposed a new piece of legislation called The Sergei Magnitsky Rule of Law Accountability Act. This would freeze assets and ban visas for those who killed Sergei as well as other Russians involved in serious human rights abuse.

Despite the White House's desire to reset relations with Russia at the time, this case shined a bright light on the criminality and impunity of the Putin regime and persuaded Congress that something needed to be done. In November 2012 the Magnitsky Act passed the House of Representatives by 364 to 43 votes and later the Senate 92 to 4 votes. On December 14, 2012, President Obama signed the Sergei Magnitsky Act into law.

Putin was furious. Looking for ways to retaliate against American interests, he settled on the most sadistic and evil option of all: banning the adoption of Russian orphans by American families.

This was particularly heinous because of the effect it had on the orphans. Russia did not allow the adoption of healthy children, just sick ones. In spite of this, American families came with big hearts and open arms, taking in children with HIV, Down syndrome, Spina Bifida and other serious ailments. They brought them to America, nursed them, cared for them and loved them. Since the Russian orphanage system did not have the resources to look after these children, many of those unlucky enough to remain in Russia would die before their 18th birthday. In practical terms, this meant that Vladimir Putin sentenced his own, most vulnerable and sick Russian orphans to death in order to protect corrupt officials in his regime.

Why did Vladimir Putin take such a drastic and malicious step?

For two reasons. First, since 2012 it's emerged that Vladimir Putin was a beneficiary of the stolen $230 million that Sergei Magnitsky exposed. Recent revelations from the Panama Papers have shown that Putin's closest childhood friend, Sergei Roldugin, a famous cellist, received $2 billion of funds from Russian oligarchs and the Russian state. It's commonly understood that Mr. Roldugin received this money as an agent of Vladimir Putin. Information from the Panama Papers also links some money from the crime that Sergei Magnitsky discovered and exposed to Sergei Roldugin. Based on the language of the Magnitsky Act, this would make Putin personally subject to Magnitsky sanctions.

This is particularly worrying for Putin, because he is one of the richest men in the world. I estimate that he has accumulated $200 billion of ill-gotten gains from these types of operations over his 17 years in power. He keeps his money in the West and all of his money in the West is potentially exposed to asset freezes and confiscation. Therefore, he has a significant and very personal interest in finding a way to get rid of the Magnitsky sanctions.

The second reason why Putin reacted so badly to the passage of the Magnitsky Act is that it destroys the promise of impunity he's given to all of his corrupt officials.

There are approximately ten thousand officials in Russia working for Putin who are given instructions to kill, torture, kidnap, extort money from people, and seize their property. Before the Magnitsky Act, Putin could guarantee them impunity and this system of illegal wealth accumulation worked smoothly. However, after the passage of the Magnitsky Act, Putin's guarantee disappeared. The Magnitsky Act created real consequences outside of Russia and this created a real problem for Putin and his system of kleptocracy.

For these reasons, Putin has stated publicly that it was among his top foreign policy priorities to repeal the Magnitsky Act and to prevent it from spreading to other countries. Since its passage in 2012, the Putin regime has gone after everybody who has been advocating for the Magnitsky Act.

One of my main partners in this effort was Boris Nemtsov. Boris testified in front of the U.S. Congress, the European Parliament, the Canadian Parliament, and others to make the point that the Magnitsky Act was a "pro-Russian" piece of legislation because it narrowly targeted corrupt officials and not the Russian people. In 2015, Boris Nemtsov was murdered on the bridge in front of the Kremlin.

Boris Nemtsov's protégé, Vladimir Kara-Murza, also traveled to law-making bodies around the world to make a similar case. After Alexander Bastrykin, the head of the Russian Investigative Committee, was added to the Magnitsky List in December of 2016, Vladimir was poisoned. He suffered multiple organ failure, went into a coma and barely survived.

The lawyer who represented Sergei Magnitsky's mother, Nikolai Gorokhov, has spent the last six years fighting for justice. This spring, the night before he was due in court to testify about the state cover up of Sergei Magnitsky's murder, he was thrown off the fourth floor of his apartment building. Thankfully he survived and has carried on in the fight for justice.

That all changed in July 2003, when Putin arrested Russia's biggest oligarch and richest man, Mikhail Khodorkovsky. Putin grabbed Khodorkovsky off his private jet, took him back to Moscow, put him on trial, and allowed television cameras to film Khodorkovsky sitting in a cage right in the middle of the courtroom. That image was extremely powerful, because none of the other oligarchs wanted to be in the same position. After Khodorkovsky's conviction, the other oligarchs went to Putin and asked him what they needed to do to avoid sitting in the same cage as Khodorkovsky. From what followed, it appeared that Putin's answer was, "Fifty percent." He wasn't saying 50 percent for the Russian government or the presidential administration of Russia, but 50 percent for Vladimir Putin personally. From that moment on, Putin became the biggest oligarch in Russia and the richest man in the world, and my anti-corruption activities would no longer be tolerated." End. (When I write End, that is the end of the excerpt) What is interesting about this testimony is Sergei's mother's lawyer was actually being subpoenaed by the defense in the trial as a witness, and Browder's side did not want him to testify under oath because he could expose Browder's lies. He is presently living in the United States, so I assume, has made a recovery. Browder's retelling of events in regard to Khodorkovsky is perplexing as well considering his direct quotes around the time of Khodorkovsky's arrest were far different. Browder's reaction to his incarceration was to say (Khodorkovsky is) "…widely credited with masterminding much of the financial trickery that plagued the Russian capital market throughout the 1990s". Other quotes from Browder given at the time of Khodorkovky's arrest were "who's next?", and "people will forget in six months that Khodorkovsky is still sitting in jail." Browder is right though that Khodorkovsky was behind a lot of the financial trickery. Khodorkovsky was so good at these auctions when a bank would sell shares of oil, gas, and minerals, he would buy the bank first to control the auctions. Khodorkovsky told a Russian reporter, Ben E., "I'm all three generations of Rockefellers rolled into one; robber baron, empire builder, and royalty." His bank, Menatep, ran some of the auctions Browder benefited from. I guess Browder's biggest prize he claimed from the auctions though was marrying a public relations spokesperson for Khodorkovsky's Yukos Oil company. Browder's siding with Putin must have been forgiven with the marriage. Khodorkovsky would go on to bankroll a lot of organizations in the West and donate heavily to both sides of the aisle in Washington D.C. *Resolution 322* that denounced Putin's jailing of Khodorkovsky was brought to the Senate floor by Joe Biden and co-sponsored by John McCain and a freshman Senator from Illinois, Barack Obama. Khodorkovsky also ran *Open Russia*. He says he named after George Soros' *Open Society* NGO. *Open Russia* is a sort of drop box, like Wikileaks, where people can send anonymous information. His son, Pavel, was also behind *The Interpreter*, an online journal that translates and analyzes Russian media. Editor in Chief of *The Interpreter*, Michael Weiss, would write favorable articles about Khodorkovsky and Browder. *Open Russia* has since changed its name to *openDemocracy*.

After Browder finished his testimony, Senator Lyndsey Graham asked him if he thought the Russian Government was behind the Trump Tower meeting. Browder giggles a bit as he went on to discuss that the Kremlin was surely aware that this meeting was taking place and speculates they were involved with its planning. We know Bill Browder knew about the meeting because he emailed a picture of Ms. Veselnitskaya's house to the State Department and to Congressional staffer, Kyle Parker, a few days before the meeting occurred. He sent the picture of her house on Monday, June 6, 2016 and the Trump Tower meeting was June 9th, 2016, three days later. So, let's face it, this woman was being monitored very closely, especially by Browder. On June 1st, 2016, there is an email from journalist, Michael Weiss, to Browder and his associate, Vadim Kleiner, saying Ms. Veselnitskaya is trying to contact Weiss on Facebook and it was "hilarious". Browder then forwards his exchange with Weiss to Kyle Parker and Robert Otto on June 7th, 2016. No one seems concerned a UK financier is sharing surveillance photos of a private Russian citizen's house to the State Department and a Congressional staffer. As Michael Weiss said in an email, "Enjoy". We aren't allowed to ask questions about this tight circle's exchanges. Browder's command over the narrative is compelling and if anyone dares ask him a challenging question, that person asking the question would be called a Russian asset for buying into Kremlin propaganda. This accusation essentially shuts down debate of anyone questioning Browder and has been used countless times by Browder and his supporters. I guess McCarthyism is OK for Bill when he goes after his opponents, but it was not OK when his grandmother was being harassed. One congressman that was heavily criticized for questioning Browder was Dana Rohrabacher from California. He was lobbied by Rinat Akhmetshin and Dana appeared receptive to learning more about the details surrounding Browder's character. Dana even met with Nataliya Veselnitskaya in Moscow, April 2016, where she talked about Browder and the contradictions in his testimony to Congress compared to her sources. Dana was supportive of Ms Veselnitskaya when she came to New York a couple of months later. He heavily promoted the documentary *The Magnitsky Act* to Congress. He tried to have the film viewed in Congress but this was denied. The Newseum was then the settled venue. Dana even tried to have the director address Congress, but as Nekrasov sat in attendance at the Congressional hearings about Russian influence in our elections, he was never called on. Nataliya Veselnitskaya was also in attendance at the hearing and sat in the front row behind former ambassador to Russia, Michael McFaul, who was addressing Congress. Later on, McFaul would over dramatize the situation saying it was frightening to have her seated next to his sons and she appeared to be looking at his laptop. Michael McFaul is a frequent critic of both the Trump administration and the Putin administration and will tweet daily about both leaders. Being smeared by the media as a Russian asset didn't deter Congressman Dana Rohrabacher from pursuing the story and he traveled to Berlin where he met with Rinat Akhmetshin April 11th, 2017 to discuss Nataliya Veselnitskaya's information about Browder. Nico Hines of the Daily Beast wrote about this visit in an article July 19th, 2017. The picture in the article is of Dana Rohrabacher with puppet strings and a large arm controlling the Dana puppet, implying Dana is a puppet for the Kremlin. Dana was up for reelection in 2018 and the ads were brutal in their criticisms calling him a Russian asset, puppet, useful idiot, etc… It was an effective campaign with videos by Journalist, Michael Weiss, chiming in with data points explaining Dana was a threat to the United States. Dana lost his campaign bid and is now a private citizen. Being out of Congress does not place him out of the spotlight of Bill Browder smears though. Browder recently tweeted out a picture of Dana exiting his Tesla with the caption "Teslas aren't cheap. Where did Dana Rohrabacher get the money for a new Tesla directly after a multi decade career as a Congressman?" Bill Browder was retweeting a political opponent of Dana's who took the candid photo of Dana getting out of the Tesla. Paul Martin wrote in the caption of his tweet in parenthesis "(Swear I heard Russian spoken)". These insinuations are very common to anyone that dares to research beyond Browder's version of events, so nothing surprises me with these accusations.

Observing the infowars surrounding those for and against Browder, I have noticed this is a consistent theme by Browder and associates to smear someone as a Russian asset if they question his narrative. Andrei Nekrasov was shocked this label was placed on him since all his documentaries have been critical of the Putin administration and he was welcomed in the anti-Putin ex pat crowd with open arms for years. In his documentary about Alexander Litvinenko, Andrei interviews Litvinenko long before his poisoning, and also in the film he interviews Boris Berezovsky and Anna Politkovskaya. These were three critics of Vladimir Putin who all had tragic deaths since the film. Anna and

Alexander were murdered, and Boris found hanging in his bathroom, his death ruled a suicide. To say Andrei Nekrasov is a Russian asset seems to be the complete opposite of his career as a filmmaker, which makes Browder's smears against the film director all the more questionable. I watched *"Rebellion"*, the documentary about Litvinenko, after I finished watching *The Magnitsky Act* and it piqued my curiosity even further to pursue the leads Nekrasov discusses in the film. I begin to spend more time on Twitter exploring the topic and there are endless amounts of sources to pursue. Endless information is part of the problem. What is accurate? What is disinformation? What is important? Am I being too bias to outliers and ignoring the truth? For months I communicate with people online trying to get questions answered. What is great about Twitter is you can ask direct questions to producers, journalists, directors, and some will respond back with answers. The first place I went to ask a question was Bill Browder and he immediately blocked me. I was surprised how quickly I was shut down, but then I began to realize he blocks anyone who asks him a challenging question. So that road to inquiry was closed. Then I talked to Torstein Grude, the producer of *The Magnitsky Act*, Andrei Nekrasov, the director of *The Magnitsky Act*, Alex Krainer, a Hedge Fund manager, who wrote a book critical of Browder, and Lucy Komisar, a Financial journalist, who investigated Bill Browder's offshore companies and his shell companies in Russia. The person I most interacted with was an American Iraq and Afghanistan war veteran named Joe. He had a unique perspective on the Browder story and had been following much longer than I had. His grandfather was a Trotskyite who left Stalin's Russia and settled in Wisconsin as a farmer. Joe, although not college educated, was extremely well read, spoke Russian, and had real world experiences that gave him insight into the narrative that very few had. I felt it was a privilege to have had these conversations with Joe and he was patient with all my questions. One day we were discussing that Browder was going to speak at a conference in New York City next month called *PutinCon* and we thought it would be interesting to hear him speak live. Joe was unable to attend but I told him I would tell him about the event if I decided to register.

I went on the *PutinCon* website and on impulse registered for the daylong event sponsored by the Human Rights Foundation, a non-profit based in New York City run by Thor Halvorssen and Garry Kasparov. It was $95 and I put it on my credit card before I changed my mind. When my husband got home from work, I mentioned I was going to attend this event and he looked at me like I had four eyes. He has been extremely patient with my new hobby researching Browder, but I could tell he was annoyed that my latest addiction took up a lot of my free time. I had become distracted in conversations giving him an "uh huh" to a question with my eyes barely lifting from my phone as I was arguing with people on Twitter. I knew this was becoming an unhealthy habit and I thought going to New York and absorbing the atmosphere may get it "out of my system." When I told my 20 year old son I was attending this event, he was genuinely concerned for my safety as Bill Browder claims to be Putin's enemy number one and his speaking in public could make him a target of an extra judicial killing. The location of the event was not yet emailed to us, out of security concerns, and we were given the general neighborhood of Hell's Kitchen for the venue, but not the exact address. I haven't attended many conferences outside of my profession as a Physical Therapist, so I was not sure how common an occurrence this was with geopolitical conferences. I assured him it would be fine, and I appreciated his concern but I wasn't worried. I woke up at 3 am and drove to the city searching for a parking garage with not much time to spare before the 9 am start. There were armed guards at the entrance with rifles who carefully watched the crowd entering the building. The venue seated 800 and appeared full, with participants mostly on the younger side, dressed in business casual. At lunch break I spoke to many who were lawyers, employees at NGOs, (non-government organizations), and journalists. All were friendly and appeared not to have any skepticism to any of the speaker's narratives. The speakers were a collection of Russian experts, Russian ex pats, and data analysts that were explaining how the 2016 election was heavily influenced by Russia. There was clearly an anti-Trump vibe throughout the day with the audience and the speakers. Garry Kasparov, the co-founder of *HRF*, was particularly critical of Trump and seemed disgruntled that Trump downplayed Russia's efforts to get him elected. I knew New Yorkers are liberal, and I was coming from Massachusetts, which is equally liberal, but I was still alarmed at the level of vitriol towards the President from many of the attendees and speakers. Of course, these would be off the cuff remarks with a wry smile, which the audience would laugh at and cheer, but I still thought this was rude. Preet Bharara, who interviewed Bill Browder for his segment at the event was also emphasizing the strong correlation between Putin, Erdogan, and Trump. He says they were three leaders who didn't like him. He wore it as badge of honor that Trump fired him and Preet and Browder were well received by the audience. This was in March of 2018, a year into the Mueller investigation, so Russian hysteria was at its peak. The speakers had me questioning if I'm a victim of Russian disinformation and I was watching documentaries that are Russian propaganda. I must have been tricked the last six months by Russia on Twitter. Andrei Nekrasov must have been fooled by the Russian government to have fallen for all their lies about Browder and Magnitsky. Eight hours of speakers told me anyone who supported Trump was influenced by Russia, and they had the data analysis to prove this. Russia has been using Wikileaks to run their disinformation campaigns like Brexit, Trump support, and even were the heavy hitters behind the recent Catalonia uprisings in Spain. Toomas Hendrick Ilves, a professor at Stanford University, put up slide after slide explaining how social media posts about Catalonia were mostly generated from Venezuela and Russia. I tried to listen to his lecture with an open mind, but I was still skeptical of the narrative he put forward. Surely the protests in Catalonia were grassroots, and the hundreds of thousands of people marching were brought out by their displeasure of the Spanish government and not from Russian and Venezuelan backed social media posts? This seemed to be more paranoia to me, but as I spoke to attendees, no one seemed to question the experts. I felt like an outlier in the crowd, a crowd full of Trump hating, Putin hating, Browder loving people. There was an anonymous blogger I followed on Twitter that I knew was attending the event that goes by the handle @jimmysllama. Definitely not a Trump supporter, but well researched on Browder's lies. She was live tweeting her reactions to the speakers, and I messaged her to meet me at break but she ignored. I suppose wishing to remain anonymous. As I looked around the lobby at break, I observed the posters and the murals along the walls. A large distorted photo of Putin and a quote from Browder was placed at the coat check that stated "Putin is terrified of losing power, and the only way he can stay in power is to turn the screws tighter on the people". Another poster had a picture of Putin as a young KGB agent with the saying, "Putin's Choice: Back to Nicholas I." The next wall over was the same picture of Putin repeated over and over, so his face was duplicated 20 times on the wall. Templates and markers were available for anyone who wanted to deface Putin's face with sayings like "bot", "thief", "kingpin" and "murderer". Some of the graffiti artists added devil horns and Hitler mustaches to his face. Not having studied Putin closely in my life, I had to default to these experts who obviously knew more about this Russian leader than myself. I have always found Putin an enigma, a leader I had neither positive or negative feelings towards, but clearly, he was poorly received at this venue. Later on I would research more on the incredibly expensive PR campaign put forth to paint Putin in a very negative light, but at the time, it was all very surreal. I drove home to Massachusetts after *PutinCon,* mulling the speakers' words over in my mind and wanting to write down my thoughts on the day. When I got home, I wrote out an editorial of my opinions on PutinCon and sent to my Twitter friend Joe, who posted on his website. His website is a collection of writings relating to Russia and Ukraine. He thanked me for my insight into the event and asked jokingly if I got my copy of

Red Notice autographed by Bill Browder. I hadn't had a chance to read the book yet, but Joe had read and asked me to have Bill write "TTs for BB", which he later told me was a story in the book about Browder being teased when he was younger at school. The kids would chase him and shout "TTs for BB!" which meant titty twisters for Bill Browder! I laughed and said I would definitely have to read the book soon then. I had read Alex Krainer's book, '*The Grand Deception, The Truth about Bill Browde*r', which was a critical analysis of Bill Browder, so I knew my initial reading of Bill Browder's book, *Red Notice*, would be a bit bias. I told Joe that Browder sat two rows in front of me at one point, so, I wasn't quite close enough for an autograph or a "TT", but I did snap some photos of Browder and Preet Bharara shaking hands at a photo op in the lobby.

After a few days being home from New York, my husband was hoping my interests in this subject had peaked, but I was more resolved than ever to find out the answers to this mystery.

Chapter 2

THE BROWDER FAMILY AND STALIN.

To REALLY DIVE deep into the psyche of Bill Browder, I felt I needed to delve into the history of the Browder family. There is extensive research done on the Browders since Bill's grandfather was a well-known historical figure in American history. His Wikipedia page is long and well documented with links to sources giving you an endless supply of articles to scour through. Earl Browder, Bill Browder's grandfather, was head of the Communist Party in America and twice ran for President of the United States against FDR in 1936 and 1940. Earl Browder was born in 1891 into a large poor family in Wichita, Kansas and had to leave school at age nine to help support his family. Early on he became a socialist and active supporter of the trade unions. When World War I had broken out he and his brother, Bill, became draft resistors opposing the war and were imprisoned in Leavenworth. This was around the time of the *1917 Espionage Act*, a federal law that made it easier to prosecute revolutionaries and resistors. While he was in prison, his family supported his draft resistance. His father wrote a poem about his sons' incarcerations titled "At the Prison Gate", which was published in the leading communist paper in America called *The Worker's World (WWP)*. After Earl's release from prison he traveled extensively to Moscow and Shanghai, organizing trade unions in China and attending Communist training camps in Russia. Earl met his wife Raisa in Russia at one of the training camps, and their first child, Felix, was born in Russia in 1927. I learned a lot about Earl from watching a lecture by his granddaughter, Laura Browder, that she gave to the University of New England Humanities department February 10, 2014. Laura is an author of several books and a professor at the Virginia Commonwealth University. She was doing a lot of researcher on her grandfather, Earl Browder, and his role in American politics, but never finished the book she intended to write about him. She was interviewed by Marie Brenner for Marie's long piece on Bill Browder published November 11th, 2018 in *Vanity Fair*. Laura educated Marie on the family's ties to Stalin and their roles as spies on different continents for NKVD. The NKVD was the old name for the secret police in the USSR between 1934 to 1943, before they became known as the KGB. When Marie Brenner asked Bill Browder about his family being spies for Stalin, Browder stated this was the first he ever heard about their role. This is somewhat surprising when you listen to Laura talk about how much she used her family as resources for researching her book. I think Marie may have been a bit skeptical about Browder not knowing this important part of his family history. She shifted gears quickly though to paint Browder as someone who struggled with his family's communist past. Bill Browder told Marie about conversations he wanted to have with his dad like, "Why did your father not renounce the atrocities of Joseph Stalin? What did it feel like to you when he was smeared during the McCarthy era?" Browder explains, "My father was not the kind of person you could ever ask any of that. He was a genius. Geniuses are lopsided. He had an I.Q of 200 and an E.Q that was a lot less. We were not a family that ever discussed feelings." This was briefly mentioned in the Vanity Fair article and the interview continued with no follow up to his lack of knowledge about the family history. Laura's lecture was very informative, and she clearly had done extensive research on the family history. She seemed proud of her grandfather, at the same time, very honest with his role as a spy for Stalin. Her grandfather's campaign slogan was "Communism is Twentieth Century Americanism" and he had banners of pictures of Marx, Lenin, and Stalin right alongside Washington, Lincoln, and Jefferson. In her research, Laura spoke to Jack Stachel's son, who explained his father was also a leader in the Communist Party in America. Jack's son said his dad came up with the slogan but because Jack had a heavy Lithuanian accent and Earl Browder had a Midwestern accent, they thought Earl would better represent the Communist Party to appeal to average Americans.

In 1995 KGB documents were declassified and Laura's father learned some of the family's history working for the NKVD. The declassification became known as the Venona papers and Earl Browder is mentioned in the papers, along with other family members. Anonymous blogger at the website, jimmysllama.com, has done great research looking into the family's history in the Venona papers. Earl Browder's alias was Rulevoj ("Helmsman") in the Venona papers. Other family members who worked with NKVD were Earl's brother, Bill Browder, his sister Marguerite, his niece Helen Lowry, Helen's husband Iskhak Akemerov, Iskhak's son, and even the nanny of Earl's children was thought to exchange information back to the Stalin government. "Nanya", knew no English, and was thought to be giving information at her church that was then delivered back to Russia. Laura Browder talks honestly about these family stories that were passed down, but she does admit both her father, and her Uncles, found it difficult to learn about the declassification of the KGB files and their father sharing secrets back to the secret police of Russia. Earl Browder's usefulness didn't last forever with Stalin, and Stalin expelled him from the Communist Party. Earl said Stalin thought his ideology of believing communism and capitalism could co exist was wrong. The Stalin government, according to Earl

The Browder Family and Stalin.

Browder, thought he was too patriotic towards America. According to Laura Browder, Earl and Raisa hung portraits of Stalin, Lenin, and Mao in their home despite the fact Stalin ordered the assassination of Raisa's first husband, the former editor of Pravda. Raisa's first husband was a Red Army General in the Soviet Army and was executed on Stalin's orders. Discussing the family's history was a touchy subject in the family and the sons of Earl were reluctant to talk about their father's relationship with Russia since he was in and out of prison during their childhood. The oldest child, Felix, was born in 1927 in Russia, shortly after Earl married Raisa, who was a Bolshevik in her youth. Felix's brother, Andrew, was born in 1931, and the last brother, Bill, was born in the U.S in 1933, after the family moved back to America. This was a time before the Soviet Nazi Pact to not invade each other's countries, and Senators and even a Supreme Court Justice were still openly sympathetic to the Communist Party, but after the 1939 Pact, there was less sympathy to the American Communist party in Washington. In fact, during this time, fellow members of the Communist Party like Stachel went underground, giving their kids new names, and trying to hide their identities. Earl, however, continued to be more active, going to Spain and giving support to the Abraham Lincoln Brigade during the Spanish civil war and continuing to promote communism in the United States. Earl was put on trial for old passport violations and sentenced to four years. His wife during this time was also threatened with deportation, despite her ill health battling cancer. Raisa was not deported and Earl ended up serving only fourteen months because at this point, Germany invaded the Soviet Union, and Earl Browder once again, began a leadership position. During Bill Browder's 2015 video deposition in the *Prevezon vs US* case in the SDNY Browder states the reason he gave up his US citizenship in 1998 was a protest for how his grandmother was persecuted by the US government during the McCarthy era.

Bill Browder's mother, Eva, had been put up for adoption in Austria and sent to America as Hitler came to power. Eva later reunited with her mother when her mother came to America. Eva would eventually become one of the first women to be accepted at M.I.T. The Browder family was wildly successful, but I'm sure the persecution of Eva's family for being Jewish, was a hardship she brought with her from her past. Laura Browder did most of her research on the family at NYU where the American Communist Party papers were stored and at Syracuse University where in the mid 1960s, Earl Browder sold all his published and unpublished writings to a book dealer, who then sold to Syracuse University. Laura also discussed the Childs brothers, Jack and Morris, who were close to Earl Browder and spied on Browder initially for the secret police for the Soviet Union, and later on for the FBI. Earl Browder never learned how to drive, and Jack was his driver when he went to visit his dad on the farm in Missouri or anywhere Earl traveled. Jack took candid pictures of the family, such as Earl's kids feeding the chickens, or lighting Earl's dad's pipe. Unbeknownst to the Browder's, Jack Childs was reporting details back to the FBI. When Laura begins to discuss her cousin, Bill Browder, she mistakenly states that the Putin government seized $230 million of Browder's assets. Actually, it was $230 million stolen from the Russian treasury with someone using Browder's companies. Browder did not lose a penny in the tax fraud. Laura seems to be a meticulous researcher and I can't help but think she is just repeating what her cousin Bill Browder must've told her in 2014, when she talked to him about his experiences in Russia. Laura wanted to go to Russia for research, but when she called up the State Department, they discouraged her from traveling to Russia because her cousin Bill was on the Interpol list to be extradited back to Russia to serve his nine year conviction sentence. When she called up Browder to get his opinion on traveling to Russia, Browder told her stories of his staff in Russia being harassed, even those who hadn't worked for him in 12 years were being harassed. Browder told Laura he had to evacuate his staff to London. He urged her not to go for safety reasons. So, Laura took Browder's advice and did not travel to Russia in the summer of

2014 to research her family's history. I do wonder if she did travel to Russia if her opinions on her cousin may have been different.

Browder was a bit of an anomaly in the family, since he didn't pursue a career in academia, but as he says, did the only thing a rebellious teenager in a family of communists could do, "put on a suit and tie and go into business". Bill Browder's father received a PhD from Princeton University at age 20 and had been honored by many administrations for his contributions to science. In 1999 Bill Clinton awarded him the National Medal of Science. Felix played a critical role in establishing multiplayer research projects that were sponsored by the intelligence community. Some of the projects included Monitoring message systems, bio surveillance data monitoring, and technology into unmanned aircraft systems. The Director Emeritus of DIMACS, Fred Roberts, stated that Felix Browder had "continued to play an important role as DIMACS grew and developed."

Felix headed the University of Chicago mathematics department for twelve years and held posts at MIT, BU, Brandeis, Yale, and finally at Rutgers University. At first it was difficult for him to obtain employment because of his father's history in the Communist Party, but Eleanor Roosevelt, who was a trustee at Brandeis University, encouraged his appointment there despite other staff being reluctant because he would create a controversial political environment. Bill Browder, his son, spoke at a recent event at University of Chicago, and reminisced about how he was a proud graduate of the University of Chicago preschool, which he attended when his father taught on campus.

Felix's brothers, William and Andrew, were also successful in academia in the mathematics departments. William Browder, Bill Browder's Uncle, was chair of the mathematic department at Princeton University from 1971 to 1973 and was President of the American Mathematical Society from 1989 to 1991. Andrew Browder, Laura's father, graduated from MIT and taught over 100 courses at different

Universities including Brown University, Berkeley, and University of California. Felix's sons, Bill and Thomas, were also highly educated, but Thomas was the one who followed in his dad and Uncle's footsteps and went into the field of academia. Thomas was a physicist specializing in the experimental study of subatomic particles. He was a professor in Hawaii who also spent much of his time in Tsukuba, Japan, working on the Belle II, an asymmetric electron-Positron Collider, nicknamed KEK. Bill Browder did not pursue a career in academics, and he has talked about his career trajectory often in TED talks, speeches on campuses, and at dozens of banquets he attends receiving awards for being a human rights advocate the world over. So, let's explore a little bit of the story of Bill Browder, once the largest foreign investor in Russia, Putin's enemy number one, and a tireless human rights advocate throughout the world.

Chapter 3

WHO IS BILL BROWDER?

BILL BROWDER WAS born in Princeton, New Jersey and grew up in Chicago. He attended University of Colorado in Boulder initially, then finished his undergraduate degree at University of Chicago with a degree in Economics. He then attended Stanford Graduate Business school and received an MBA. After graduating from business school, he moved to London. Browder started his London career in the Eastern European practice of the Boston Consulting Group, then he worked for Robert Maxwell's MCC conglomerate, and after that, managed the Russian investment desk for Salomon Brothers. After Salomon Brothers, Browder founded Hermitage Capital Management in 1996, receiving his seed capital of $25 million from Edmund Safra for the purpose of investing in Russia during the mass privatization after the fall of the Soviet Union. Benny Steinmetz was also an original investor in Hermitage. Browder bought shares in Russian oil companies Gazprom and Surgutneftegaz, and other companies including RAO, UES, Sberbank, Sidanco, Avisma, and Volzhanka.

In 1999 Browder sold his Titanium company, Avisma, and the

new owners turned around and filed a RICO against Browder and other previous Avisma investors, including Kenneth Dart. The new owners alleged Browder illegally siphoned company assets into offshore accounts and then transferred the fund to U.S. accounts at Barclays before the purchase. Browder and his codefendants settled with Avisma in 2000. They sold their Avisma shares as part of the confidential settlement agreement. In March 2013, HSBC, a bank that serves as the trustee and manager of Hermitage Capital Management, announced that it would end the fund's operations in Russia. The decision was taken amid two legal cases against Browder and his convictions in absentia for tax evasion in Moscow. This was reported by Bloomberg at the time of the announcement.

On July 13th, 2013, Browder was convicted nine years for large scale tax evasion of 522 million rubles. Sergei Magnitsky's family was denied rehabilitation for Magnitsky crimes in Kalmykia with shell companies Saturn and Dalnaya Step, but Sergei was not convicted since deceased. If the family did not request rehabilitation, his case would have been closed upon death. In December 29, 2017 Browder was convicted an additional nine years for large scale tax evasion of 3 billion rubles or 45.3 million dollars. Ivan Cherkasov was also found guilty in absentia for the same crimes involving the company Kameya and other LLCs. In June 2018, HSBC offered a settlement with Russian government for 17 million pounds for its part in the alleged tax avoidance through Browder's companies, but Russia refused this offer and the case is still being negotiated.

"Browder's earlier settlement agreement with Avisma, seemed to indicate a long-standing habit of siphoning off funds to offshore accounts. He also had been found guilty of evading some $40 million in taxes by using fake deductions." This is a paragraph on his Wikipedia page and I see the brilliant financial investigative reporter, Lucy Komisar, may have snuck this on Browder's Wikipedia page. I hope so anyways. She originally started researching Browder after Mikhail Khodorkovsky sold Avisma to Browder and Browder then sold to a Russian businessman who turned around and sued Browder. Lucy has done great interviews on a radio program *Fault Lines* and another podcast, *Around the Empire,* discussing the Avisma case in greater detail. Also jimmysllama.com has an excellent article on her website explaining the Avisma case and Browder's financial dealings with Khodorkovsky.

In the past several years Bill Browder has received many awards including from *GQ* magazine, as one of the "men of the year in 2017". In 2018 he was named the 67th most powerful person in the world by *Worth* magazine noting "Browder has become one of the biggest thorns in Putin's side, and appears to be a key reason Russia interfered in the 2016 U.S Presidential election". Browder's interview with Preet Bharara on the *"Stay Tuned with Preet"* podcast received the *People's Choice Webby award* for Best Individual Podcast. Also in 2018 he received the *Aspen Institute Henry Crown Leadership Award*, a prize honoring "an outstanding leader whose achievements reflect the high standards of integrity, industry, and philanthropy". Previous awardees include Colin Powell, Jimmy Carter, Jeff Bezos, and Madeline Albright. Then in 2019 he received the *Lantos Human Rights Prize* for his role as the "driving force behind the Magnitsky Sanctions, the most consequential enforcement mechanism of the modern human rights movement." Previous awardees have included the Dalai Lama, Elie Wiesel, Hillary Clinton, and Shimon Peres. Don't forget he also was awarded the *American Spirit Award for Citizen Activism.* Previous awardees have included General David Petraeus, John McCain, and Fareed Zakaria. Quite an impressive award for a guy who in 1998, gave up his U.S citizenship in protest of the treatment his grandmother received during the 1950s. I guess he wasn't feeling the right "American Spirit" back then.

So how does a Hedge Fund manager, who says he was kicked out of Russia in 2005, become the recipient of dozens and dozens of awards and honors? This is the story we will journey to uncover.

Chapter 4

BROWDER GOES TO MOSCOW

THE EASIEST THING to do would be to believe Browder is a trustworthy character and all these accolades bestowed on him make him worthy of these lofty merits. But there are too many lies unsurfaced that make me question if he is even lying about what he ate for breakfast. I'm going to spend the rest of this book pouring over all the accusations by the Russian Federation towards Browder and scrutinize his book Red Notice. If you want to end your journey here, I don't blame you. In fact, I highly recommend it because it makes the world a much simpler place. Russia is bad. America is good. Browder is a beacon of truth and righteousness. The End.

No need to question the chosen narrative put forth by the mainstream media. No need to be called a Russian asset for even peeking behind the curtain of Browder's fairytales.

Browder is a fascinating character. Every time I read a new article or tweet he puts out, I try to imagine he is genuinely a sincere person, but this is a very difficult task based on all the research I have done cross checking his accusations with other sources. I have been observing his media manipulation the past couple of years and also looking at past manipulation, when he carved out his narrative most of the world knows from his book *Red Notice*. Browder describes how he fed stories to the media by breaking the story into seven chapters and giving one chapter to each newspaper. He also would describe how he would give a newspaper an exclusive story and tell them if they didn't run it in 48 hours, he was going to give the story to another newspaper as well. The media always wanted an exclusive story, so this would motivate the newspaper to print exactly what Browder wanted, since there was no time to research. Browder would sometimes take these stories he spoon-fed to the media and use these stories as proof to say a company was corrupt, or a person was an asset to Russia. Often, he would use dead whistleblowers as his only source. A journalist would print this at face value, and Browder would quote the article the journalist wrote. This "intel laundering" allowed character assassinations of whoever he wanted.

So, let's go over Browder's career starting with financial investor turned human rights crusader, and see if his Road to Damascus moment began the day his tax accountant, Sergei Magnitsky, was thrown into a Russian jail. Browder begins his financial career at an interesting time, exactly when the Berlin Wall came down in 1989 and Russia and other countries behind the Soviet bloc were trying to transition from communism under the USSR, to being self-sufficient countries introducing capitalism. Browder's first job out of college was working at Boston Consulting Group. This brought him to Poland to invest in the newly privatized companies as the Free Market was opening up after the breakup of the Soviet Union. Browder reminisces at a November 4th, 2009 Stanford Business school speech, that he had an interest in working in Eastern Europe upon graduation and searched and searched but could not find any opportunities. "Not a single person he knew anywhere in the world had an interest in working in former communist countries and doing business in Eastern Europe". Everyone would ask him, 'Why do you want to do that?'" When he started at Boston Consulting Group's London office as his first job, he asked an eccentric BCG partner if he could work in Eastern Europe. The partner stated they did not do business in Eastern Europe, but if they ever did, Browder could be head of their Eastern European practice. Browder receives laughter from the Stanford business school students and he smiles and proceeds to tell about his experiences. As soon as the first opportunity came to work in Eastern Europe, he was sent to the Poland/Ukrainian border to restructure a bus factory business six hours by car from Warsaw. The World Bank was looking for consultants in managing the bus factory restructuring, and BCG was awarded the contract and Bill Browder was sent to Poland. Browder recommends laying off 90% of the Polish workers and nonchalantly transitions his speech into discovering the goldmine of privatization of companies the Polish government was starting. He says he asked his Polish translator what were all these numbers in the newspaper and his translator told him they were the first available companies the public could invest in as the Polish government was transitioning from all State-owned companies under communism to attempts at ownership of companies with private citizens. Now, listening to this Stanford speech, I was struck by his callousness towards the laid off workers at the bus factory and his giddiness to the prospect of earning "easy money".

Browder states the Polish newspaper was showing seven companies that were being sold at half the value of their one-year previous earning. Yes, Browder insists he figured out this golden opportunity to invest in these companies by painstakingly having his translator help him read a Polish newspaper's section on money. This story is also outlined in Browder's book Red Notice, and this is the first time of dozens of times, I'm expected to just "believe" Browder's version of events. Well, I'm not a number's person, but to me these Forrest Gump moments that happen over and over to Bill Browder seem to be fabrications that are not based in reality. To me, the more plausible scenario would be this first-year associate was receiving assistance from other entities, either other employees at BCG, the World Bank, or possibly even a country's government. Browder took his life savings of four thousand bucks and converted to Polish Zloty and bought shares in the first privatizations of Polish companies. The shares went up 10 times over the next 12 months. At this point Browder smiles and states "If you ever have made 10 times your money on anything, you'll know that it releases a certain chemical in your body" The audience loves this line and you hear hearty laughter as the camera stays fixed on Browder during the speech. This speech was only eleven years ago but Browder was much thinner than he is now in the year 2020. He is forty-five years old during the speech. He kept his hair longer on the sides unlike now where he cuts very short making the contrast between his hair and balding crown more subtle. He has on a suit and is wearing glasses and seems slightly nervous speaking in front of the crowd with a frequent stammer that is still prevalent in his speech pattern in videos I have watched. After the laughter dies down, Browder with a smirk states "and you want that chemical release again" and this line receives even more laughter. Browder states he knew he found his vocation at this moment, "of buying into privatizations in Eastern Europe". Fast forward a couple of years and Browder switches jobs to become an Investment banker at Salomon Brothers. Salomon Brothers doesn't exist anymore as it was absorbed by Citigroup. Browder describes working at Salomon Brothers as a dog-eat-dog place and recommends reading *"Liar's Poker"* by Michael Lewis, to help understand the competitive culture that exists in investment banking. He describes he had no training program, no mentors, and on his first day his boss said he had to earn five times his salary for the firm, or he would be fired. He doesn't mention a timeframe he has to earn this in, but you get a sense that the atmosphere for getting contracts in privatization in Eastern Europe is competitive. His first contract he tried to get in on was the privatization of a Hungarian Airline, but none of the other investors would let him into their contracts so he was scrambling to find an opportunity to invest in Eastern Europe that wasn't already taken. Other investors would kick him out of a board meeting because he wasn't on their privatization team and he was becoming desperate for an opportunity with the fear of being fired always lurking in his mind. He then came up with the idea to go to Russia in 1992 because none of the other Salomon Brothers employees were trying to protect their turf in Russia. In fact, when he announced this was where he was going to begin his privatization adventures, he was laughed at by the other investment bankers at Salomon Brothers. Again, this is Browder's version of events about what happened and this "aww shucks poor me" shtick comes off to me as disingenuous, but it seems to play very well to his audience. Browder starts his adventure in Russia in what he describes as "a first bite of a mandate and it was a fishing fleet located in Murmansk which was 300 miles north of the arctic circle". The company was the Murmansk trawling fleet and it was having some kind of dispute with somebody buying their fish. The trawling company hired Cleary Gottlieb, a big New York law firm, to settle this dispute. Gottlieb recommended Murmansk trawling hire an investment banker to advise them on privatization and they awarded the contract to Salomon Brothers, and thus, Bill Browder claims, he became the head, and only investment banker in Russia. He was offered $50,000 a month for two months of consulting and he states "there isn't an investment banker in the world who would get out of bed for this fee" but he was desperate, so he took the gig. "The inventory was 100 ships worth $20 million each brand new, so there was initially 2 billion worth of ships, maybe 7 years old and so, half depreciated, so a billion dollars worth of ships. Browder was hired to decide whether the management should exercise their right under the privatization program to purchase 51% of this fleet for two and a half million dollars." Browder jokes this was an easy assignment and of course Murmansk should purchase the fleet. Browder states he got the same high he got from making easy money like he did in Poland and instead of going back to London right away, he flew to

Moscow to check out the availability of other privatization opportunities. He found an English-speaking yellow pages and started cold calling people and within the course of a week, set up 30 meetings to talk about investment opportunities in the privatization sell offs in Moscow. He learned they had vouchers that the Russian Government gave to every person in the country. "So, say there were 150 million people in the country, and each voucher cost $20 dollars and that was exchangeable for 30 percent of all the shared capital of all shares in Russia. This meant the entire value of Russia in 1992 was $10 billion dollars for the whole country". "All the oil, all the gas, all the metals, all the everything, $10 billion dollars." At this point Browder describes how the adrenaline was pumping through his system as it was clear that this was just the most unbelievable opportunity ever. Browder also describes a story of how, not knowing any Russian, he buys a $5 database off a kid on the streets in Moscow with the help of his driver translating the money transaction. It just happened to be a lot of the financial data analysis he needed about the financial statements of companies that were privatizing. Gee whiz! How lucky can one guy be? After he leaves Moscow with this new knowledge, he goes back to the London office of Salomon Brothers, and tells his boss they are wasting all his time on this advisory stuff and he needed to invest in the privatization program to make the big money. He tells his boss "We should get in there, buy all this stuff, and make a fortune. They are giving it away. Gold for free." No one at Salomon Brothers was interested and Browder says he quickly became an outcast in the London office. One day he got a call from someone in the New York office saying they heard Browder might have something interesting to share about investing in Russia and an "eccentric" investor, Bobby Ludwig, gave him $25 million to invest in Russia. Again, at this point in listening to Browder describe this story to the Stanford graduate business students, and I'm struck by two things; One, is it really believable he was the only investment banker from Salomon Brothers in Russia? And two, was it believable a first-year employee would be summoned to New York for their advice on investing in Russia? As consumers of Browder's story, we are supposed to suspend disbelief and swallow his story wholesale, but I have intentions of researching Salomon Brothers investing in Russia in 1992 and also researching the privatization program at the time called "Shock Therapy". Browder talks about how he was meeting with the bigwigs of Wall Street like Edmund Safra, John Templeton, and George Soros and giving them advice on investing in Russia when he was only in his late 20s. Browder made enormous money on this privatization deal for Salomon Brothers but he realized he was only getting a salary and missing out on the opportunities for himself to personally make a lot of money. So he quit Salomon Brothers and started his own Hedge Fund company called The Hermitage Fund. Browder got the owner of The Republic National Bank of New York, Edmund Safra, to invest $25 million into his fund as an anchor investor. Browder described Safra as "a legend" in the world of private banking. So, Browder moves to Moscow in 1996, bringing his wife, Melanie, and their son, Joshua with him, leaving London, to begin to live in Moscow investing his initial $25 million. After a while his wife moves back to London with their son as she found it difficult to live in Russia. He says he went back to London every ten days to be with his son, Joshua. He describes how he invested the money in companies that didn't have Suisse Credit reports because they were valued at one tenth the value as the companies the brokers from Wall Street had written reports on. Even though the companies were the exact same products. The only difference was they hadn't received a stamp of approval yet by the West. Browder states he was the only principal investor in the West, so he had an enormous advantage over the principal investors that were physically in New York. One thing Browder fails to mention is when he is buying all these shares of companies, say in Gazprom Oil, he is doing so illegally. Lucy Komisar, a Loeb award winning financial journalist, who has been studying Browder's financial transactions for nearly two decades, explains how Browder cheats the Russian government by buying the Gazprom oil shares at a Russian resident rate when he should have been buying at the nonresident rate. On her website, TheKomisarScoop.com, Lucy will describe the financial trickery needed to pull off this tax fraud. Browder was in Moscow on a tourist visa and therefore, was not a resident of Russia. The voucher system was set up for Russian citizens and they were protected by foreign investors by a law that stated non-Russians had to buy the shares through the ADRs in London or coincidentally, The Republic Bank of New York, for one and a half times the rate Russian citizens paid. ADR's were American Depository Receipts. Browder used shell companies in Russia under the guise of ownership by Russian citizens to purchase the shares at Russian citizen rates. Many Russian citizens who did not understand the voucher program were selling their shares for cheap to buy groceries or other items and Browder would buy these bundled shares at fixed auctions. Later, Russia demanded he pay them back for his purchasing of shares illegally. It wasn't until the beginning of 2006, when it became legal for outside investors to move their stocks outside the physical boundaries of Russia. It also became legal to allow outside investors to own up to 49% of the company. Basically, what he was doing before illegally, now became legal. Browder, along with roughly 22 other oligarchs, like Mikhail Khodorkovsky, ran the privatization programs in Russia. Browder became the largest foreign investor in Russia with a fund of 4.5 billion dollars. The buying and selling of shares in Russia in the 90s would make Chicago in the 1920s look like a pre-school. There was asset stripping, embezzlement, transfer pricing, and whatever corruption you could dream up to gobble up the assets in Russia. Browder would claim he was fighting the corruption while he was investing calling it "The Hermitage Effect". He states after he reported the corruption of a company to the front pages of friendly Russian newspapers, Vladimir Putin and the Russian government would swoop in and attempt to control the corrupt, crooked oligarchs and start arresting them. For years Browder sang Putin's praises saying, "I'd trust Putin any day of the week". In 2003 when Mikhail Khodorkovsky was arrested, Browder was quoted as saying, "A nice well-run authoritarian regime is better than an oligarchic mafia regime and those are the choices on offer." Browder and MBK, as Mikhail is commonly referred to, have a long history together and Browder was either supporting him or opposing him depending on which way the wind was blowing. When Putin put MBK on trial in 2005, Browder criticized the jailed oligarch for the same asset stripping Browder profited from before, telling the BBC "Mr Khodorkovsky is no martyr. He has left in his wake aggrieved investors too numerous to count and is widely credited with masterminding much of the financial trickery that plagued the Russian capital markets throughout the 1990s." In the same year Browder told the New York Times "Putin cares about foreign investors; he just doesn't care about them enough to allow one oligarch to use his ill-gotten gains to hijack the state for his own economic purposes." However, in their earlier relationship in 1997, Browder aligned his investments with the Yukos Oil oligarch, and defended the way Yukos stripped investors and its subsidiaries to enrich the Yukos parent company. Browder stated, "When a company does terrible things to the subsidiary, I would rather be on the side of power." This on again off again relationship would solidify into an on again relationship after Browder was kicked out of Russia and MBK was released from jail. They would collaborate on lobbying around the world to put pressure on Putin's government. Both had their reasons for this pressure, but the symbiotic relationship was beneficial to both investors now turned human rights crusaders the world over.

We know Browder knew all the tricks on how to avoid taxes. In fact, in 1998 he gave up his US citizenship right around the time the US began enforcing taxing the investments of US citizens overseas . Only he knows the true reasons why he renounced, but I'm more prone to think it had something to do with saving millions on taxes. He was written up in a CBS article titled "5 citizens who left the US to avoid paying taxes", so who really knows. Browder would paint himself as the good oligarch and the other investors as the bad oligarchs depending on his relationship with them at a given time. Browder claimed Putin and the Russian government came in and cleaned up the corruption in the companies after Browder exposed the illegality. The value of the company would go up since everyone wanted to invest in a company that didn't have the profits getting stolen by a crooked oligarch. Browder would describe this as "activism investing" and he continued to see Hermitage Fund grow in value. Browder said when he worked this "activism investing", "lighting the Moscow night on fire", Putin would fire the head of Gazprom and other directors of companies such as Unified Energy Systems, Sberbank, the National Savings Bank, and Surgutneftegaz. At this point personally, his first marriage to Melanie ended in divorce, and he had married Elena. They would have two children together. Elena continued her public relations work for Yukos Oil, Khodorkovky's company. Hmmm, can you see how Khodorkovsky's name got snuck into the Magnitsky Act? With D.C insider, Jonathan Winer, your lawyer and lobbyist, and Khodorkovsky's as well, you start to see the wheels that turned behind the scenes in the halls of Congress.

Getting back to the Stanford speech that Browder gives less than two weeks before Sergei Magnitsky died, he speaks for about a half hour about money, money, money, and then the last ten minutes of the lecture he plays a video his company produced after he claims he was denied entry to Russia. This video is the story of his companies being stolen and used as vehicles to steal from the Russian treasury. It wasn't until the last thirty seconds of the ten minute video that a picture of Magnitsky is shown stating how he was being detained in a Russian prison. What struck me as odd about Browder's Stanford speech, was how not once did Browder mention Sergei, or express concern about his detention, apart from this little blip at the end of the video titled "Law and Order". Later on, I find out that Browder made no initiation to contact Sergei or Sergei's lawyers throughout Sergei's detention. Also, no reports were ever submitted to any human rights organization complaining of his eleven-month pretrial detention. Browder admits under sworn video deposition in the Prevezon case he didn't remember if anyone on his staff attempted to contact Sergei Magnitsky or Sergei's lawyers. Another big omission I discovered from his stump speeches and his book *Red Notice* is the omission of the extensive investments Salomon Brothers were doing in Russia when he was supposedly the first investor in the country. Their investment into privatization and consultation certainly didn't start with a fleet of fishing trawlers as Browder would like you to imagine. It's these deflections that make you question why he doesn't mention them, since it was a significant chapter in the corruption scandals with Salomon Brothers. Glenn Simpson, a former WSJ reporter, and now partner in an opposition research firm called Fusion GPS, would discover this omission as well. In sworn testimony to the Senate Judiciary Committee, Glenn discusses his findings. Fusion GPS was hired by the law firm, Baker Hostetler, to obtain research on Browder for their client, Denis Katsyv, who they were representing in the *Prevezon vs US* case in New York. As you know from me stating earlier, Katsyv was also represented by his Russian lawyer, Nataliya Veselnitskaya, who attended the now infamous Trump Tower meeting. She met with Glenn Simpson before and after the Trump Tower meeting to discuss the Prevezon case they were both involved in that was taking place in New York the same week. Here is an excerpt of what Glenn Simpson had to say.

BY THE WITNESS: (Glenn Simpson)

A. I'll just finish with one last thing and I'm happy to answer that question.

So in the course of this, you know — I mean, one of my interests or even obsessions over the last decade has been corruption in Russia and Russian kleptocracy and the police state that was there. I was stationed in Europe from 2005 to 2007 or '8. So I was there when Putin was consolidating power and all this wave of power was coming. So it's been a subject that I've read very widely on and I'm very interested in the history of Putin's rise.

You know, in the course of all this I'll tell you I became personally interested in where Bill Browder came from, how he made so much money under Vladimir Putin without getting involved in anything illicit. So I read his book and I began doing other research and I found filings at the SEC linking him quite directly and his company, Salomon Brothers at the time, to a company in Russia called Peter Star, and I had, as it happens, vetted Peter Star and I knew that Peter Star was, you know, at the center of a corruption case that I covered as a reporter at the Wall Street Journal. When I went back into the history of Peter Star, I realized that Bill Browder did business with the mayor's office in Saint Petersburg when Vladimir Putin was the deputy mayor and was responsible for dealing with western businessmen and corporations.

I then went and looked in Red Notice, this was a large deal, it was the biggest deal ever for Salomon at that time, they sold $98 million worth of stock on NASDAQ. There's no mention of William Browder's deal with Peter Star in Red Notice. I can't tell you why, but I can tell you that Peter Star later became the subject of a massive corruption investigation, Pan-European, that I exposed a lot of and that led to the resignation of Putin's telecoms minister. So I assume he might not have — this is kind of a pattern with Browder, which is he tends to omit things that aren't helpful to him, and I think we've seen a good bit of that lately in his allegations against me, which I'm sure you're going to ask me about.

So your question about the ICE agent, he was deposed by John Moscow of the New York office of Baker Hostetler. John is an old associate of mine from my days as a journalist. John's an expert on tax evasion and money laundering. He was the head of the rackets bureau for the district attorney's office in New York." (End of excerpt)

This testimony is fascinating and worthy of more research as it ties into the relationship that Browder may have had with Putin early on in 1992 in Russia. As we know, Browder would call Putin the biggest ally to Western Investors, so why did their relationship turn sour? Going from, "I would trust Putin any day of the week", to, "Putin's enemy number one", is quite the turn around. In fact, because Browder starts his story in Northern Russia and not St Petersburg, this deflection continues to be an interest of mine. In a panel discussion at a convention in Las Vegas in 2019, Michael McFaul and Bill Browder discussed their experiences in Russia. This was at the SALT convention, a meet and greet put on by hedge fund investor, Anthony Scaramucci. At the beginning of the panel discussion, McFaul, the former ambassador to Russia under Obama, reminisced about when they first met and says it was in St Petersburg in 1992. Browder begins to stammer and quickly changes the subject to "how another thing they have in common was both being banned from Russia". I had kept a copy of the conversation, but unfortunately, the SALT website has deleted the video, so I am unable to access the video or get a written transcript of the exchange. I mean, his logo, and the name of his company, are for a museum in St Petersburg, not a fishing fleet in Northern Russia, so it's kind of obvious. After researching Putin's career around this time, it is interesting how Putin himself was caught up in the minerals for food scandal that almost got him fired from his government position as an official in the Mayor's office in 1992. Of course, this scandal did not follow Putin to his next government jobs, and it appears both the West and Putin are happy to not draw attention to some of the corruption that occurred during this time period.

Chapter 5

RENAISSANCE VS HERMITAGE

BROWDER WOULD CONTINUE to have many interactions with fellow businessmen and politicians, and he continued to build his Hermitage Fund company. When he talks about his business dealings in his book, I begin to focus on the ones that just don't sound authentic and seem like a forced narrative. The anonymous blogger that runs the website jimmysllama.com wrote an excellent piece about Browder's relationship with another American founded company in Russia, called Renaissance Capital. I'm just going to copy the description "Jimmy" writes, because it's outstanding research.

From @Jimmysllama website: **"After opening his own firm in 1996, Browder enjoyed his luxurious lifestyle well into the next year with few if any bumps in the road. However, things were about to change Hermitage Capital got involved with Russia oil giant Sidanco. What happened was that after Browder realized the company was vastly underpriced he purchased a large block of stock in the company but failed to predict Sidanco CEO Russian oligarch Vladimir Potanin would attempt a "dilutive share issue" one year** later. Simply put, a dilutive share issue would have meant massive financial losses for Browder, his partners Edmond Safra and Beny Steinmetz, and other investors.

According to Browder's book, after hearing the news about the share issue he approached Vladimir Potanin's financial advisor and head of investment bank Renaissance Capital, Boris Jordan, at a New Year's Eve party to sort out the issue. Jordan reassured Browder and asked that he stop by Renaissance a few days later. He did and the following is an alleged conversation that took place between Browder and one of Renaissance's associates, Leonid Rozhetskin (taken from Browder's Red Notice, emphasis is Browder's):

Browder: "If this dilution goes forward, it's going to cost me and my investors- including Edmond Safra- eighty-seven million dollars."

Rozhetskin: "Yes, we know. That's the intention, Bill."

Browder: "What?"

Rozhetskin: "That's the intention."

Browder: "You're deliberately trying to screw us?"

Rozhetskin "Yes"

Step one: Contact Potanin's partners such as George Soros, the Harvard University Endowment and others and tell them about the dilutive share issue.

Step two: Contact journal friends who will write up a nice exposé

Step three: Contact the chairman of the Russian Federal Securities Commission (FSEC), Dmitry Vasiliev.

Surprisingly, the third step worked and in February, 2008, the

FSEC halted the share issue but as cut and dry as this story might sound there's more to it than meets the eye. Take Renaissance Capital for example. Founded in 1995 by Boris Jordan (the one who spoke with Browder at the New Year's Eve party) and Stephen Jennings, it's been said they employed "a string of KGB spies." Furthermore, it's the same company that paid Bill Clinton half a million dollars for a speech while promoting the Uranium One deal in Russia. You may also recall that the @thehill recently reported Bill Clinton requested clearance from the State Department to meet with Arkady Dvorkovich, a board director of Rosatom (which subsequently purchased Uranium One) during this time period, but, interestingly enough, he ended up meeting with Putin instead.

The other curious thing about Renaissance Capital is that in July 2009, Browder accused the company of being involved in the $230 million tax refund theft that led to the death of Sergei Magnitsky and, of course, the Magnitsky Act. Lo and behold, eight years later on April 13, 2017, The Telegraph ran a story reporting that the U.S government had linked part of the stolen tax refund money to Renaissance Capital. Eight years later. I mean, what? And don't ask me what it means because all I know at this point is that something obviously doesn't smell right.

Then there's the whole ex-Mossad bodyguard drama and "Omg, Potanin is going to kill me" storyline which I'm not sure I'm buy either and here's why:

Browder's partner, Edmond Safra, sent armed Israeli guards and armored cars to protect Browder while he fought Sidanco's share dilution, right? Right. And remember how Boris Jordan's associate at Renaissance Capital allegedly (told) Browder that they were purposely trying to screw him? Well, one could speculate from this information-which might I remind you came directly from Browder's book-that Renaissance, Sidanco, and Potanin were probably pretty peeved at Browder after they lost the share dilution case. I mean, let's be honest, no Russian oligarch likes to lose to a greedy, jackass of an American like Bill Browder (he was still a U.S. citizen at that point) so I think it's safe to say that Browder had room to be more concerned about his safety after Sidanco lost the case.

But he wasn't. Not in the least.

In Andrew Meier's book, Black Earth: A Journey Through Russia After the Fall, Meier wrote about a dinner he had sometime after August 1998, with Bill Browder, Peter Derby, Charlie Ryan, and….wait for it…Renaissance Capital CEO Boris Jordan. The dinner, which consisted of "snails and caviar, king prawns, and medallions of New Zealand lamb", lasted for over three hours during which time the five men discussed what had gone wrong in Russia (the dinner took place after the economic collapse of 1998). And if you are still trying to wrap your brain around the fact that Browder was enjoying a leisurely five-star meal with head of the financial company behind Sidanco, join the club. That's not to say that Browder and Jordan didn't spar over the evening's delicacies, they did. Take for instance this amazing burn by Jordan,

Browder: "This country's (Russia) so corrupt they fucked themselves."

Jordan: "Bill, you obviously don't believe that or else you didn't do your fiduciary duty for your clients, investing a billion in the place."

Ohhhh snap. And as much as I'd like to think that Browder's Israeli bodyguards were keeping watch at the door and that Jordan and Browder fought all night in order for me to reconcile Browder's narrative and Sidanco with this private dinner, according to Meier the dinner ended with discussions about "the price of bodyguards, the best tax havens for billionaires, and the travails of Bermudan citizenship." Of course it did.

Besides these guys being obvious douchebags, again, why in the world would Browder be having dinner with Potanin's financial advisor who had recently been involved in trying to screw Browder out of a shiz ton of money...that and the bodyguards, the submachine guns, and armored cars. I reached out to the author to see if I could get a specific date for the dinner because all I could deduce from the book was that it happened sometime after August, 1998 and before the author left Russia which was sometime between 1999-2000. Unfortunately, the author's only response was that he didn't have his notes with him and that "Whatever the book has would be correct." I pointed out to him that the book didn't mention a date but Meier never responded. That was over two months ago."(End of @jimmysllama excerpt)

This research done by jimmysllama.com will be very important as we progress on with Browder's adventures in the Wild West of Russia. Open sources will vastly contradict court filings in New York, the book *Red Notice*, and articles written by journalists sympathetic to Browder, like *OCCRP* and Michael Weiss of *The Daily Beast*. It is so difficult to untangle the narrative because Browder has thrown so many accusations around that have not stood up in any court of law. In fact, judges on many continents have thrown out his filings over and over because the accusations are not admissible, but Browder doesn't care. He got the headlines he wanted, and court rulings are quietly made in back pages, in small writing years later.

Browder took his "feud" with Renaissance Capital stateside with many smear articles about the company on the OCCRP website, claiming they stole the $230 million. Then OCCRP switched gears and went after Prevezon claiming brazenly their subsidiaries, Bristol Export and Nominex, received the "blood money". No proof, just arrows pointing from banks to LLCs. The testimony in the Prevezon case is comical with Browder attempting circular intel for his evidence connecting Katsyv (Prevezon) to the Russian treasury theft. Remember Natalia Veselnitskaya is one of the Prevezon lawyers. Browder cites OCCRP as his source. The Prevezon lawyer's questions and Browder's answers are examples of the entire seven hours of deposition.

Q: "They had records?
A: Yes

Q: They had records of Prevezon Holdings account and USB?
A: No

Q: So how did your team trace those funds?
A: I don't know.

(USB was one of two banks the treasury money was deposited into December 2007)

So Browder feeds OCCRP data, then tries to use this data in court stating he doesn't know how OCCRP came to these conclusions. Judge Griesa is not impressed and dismisses much of Browder's evidence as inadmissible. (OCCRP is "Organized Crime and Corruption Reporting Project", funded by George Soros and USAid as well as other contributors)

Browder originally goes after Renaissance Capital in the New York courts but drops that case after Magnitsky dies and goes after Prevezon and Katsyv instead. Renaissance Capital and Hermitage Capital Management ran in the same circles for years. Former UK ambassador to Russia, Andrew Wood, would organize seminars on how to invest in Russia and would have representatives from both companies speak back to back. First, Vadim Kleiner from Hermitage Capital, then someone from Renaissance. Sir Andrew Wood has been an advisory board member of Renaissance Capital. Browder submitted court filings to the Federal Court in the Southern District of New York subpoenaing

Renaissance bank statements and accusing them of being involved in the $230 million dollar tax refund fraud in Russia. OCCRP and Michael Weiss of the Daily Beast wrote up articles showing Renaissance Capital was responsible for Hermitage's stolen companies and the Russian treasury theft. Browder would then quietly drop pursuing these charges after Sergei Magnitsky dies, and pursues Denis Katsyv and his Real Estate Holdings company instead. Why he dropped the petition on one company and pursued on another company no one really knows, and it can only be speculation. When I say Browder was pursuing the Prevezon case, it was technically the United States government, but Browder hand delivers the case to the New York office. He was also giving podcasts with the Attorney General overseeing the case at the time, Preet Bharara, so it was his baby. This is the reason I believe he was using the courts for his own personal grievances.

Chapter 6

BROWDER GETS KICKED OUT OF RUSSIA

So, now that Maxwell is dead from falling off his yacht *"Lady Ghislane"*, and Safra has died from a fire his ex-Green Beret nurse set in his Monaco mansion, Browder keeps moving along with new investors. With Edmund Safra and Beny Steinmetz no longer his primary investors, Ziff media become his primary clients and they set up shell companies in America named Speed wagon 1 and Speed wagon 2 that receive money from Hermitage investments in Russia. Russian attorney, Nataliya Veselnitskaya, will uncover these companies during her research into Browder for her case defending her client, Denis Katsyv, from U.S charges. Browder has set up so many shell companies throughout the world that it is hard to keep track and it gets very convoluted. Let's start with two of his shell companies in Kalmykia, Russia, that come under scrutiny by the local officials. An investigation opens up on Sergei Magnitsky and Bill Browder for tax fraud and forgery using these two companies in 2004. Bill Browder continues to be non-compliant with paying the fees placed on these companies, and eventually a civil case turns into a criminal case. A more diplomatic term for these PO Box companies is Hermitage Capital subsidiaries, but as we shall see, "shell" is a more accurate description. They exist only on paper. There are no offices, no desks, no employee meetings, just an address. Then the stocks will go through what is called "money layering", where it will rinse through many other "subsidiaries" with names difficult to retain. Just remember the name Saturn to keep it simple. So, basically the scam was, they would buy Russian stocks (illegally as we discovered as non-Russian citizens), funnel through Cyprus, back to Southern Russia and any appreciation paid on the taxes was lowered because over 50% of the employees qualified under a tax break. (Tax breaks were given to the disabled in the Kalmykia region.) Employees were described as Expert analysts. The courts ruled Browder's shell companies didn't meet standards and needed to pay their fair share of taxes. Hermitage appealed and lost the case, but they were still non-compliant with paying their taxes. Browder knew he was under investigation, but was brazen enough to ignore his bills, because he was still on good terms with Putin. In fact, in Davos that year, he joked that doing business in Russia was fair, as long as you paid your taxes to Putin. It would be months later he states he was denied entry into the country, labeled as a National Security threat, so the irony of his Davos speech is especially strong. There is some confusion if even this part of his story is true, because his associate says Browder was denied entry in 2008, three years later after he says he was kicked out. His associate is Paul Wrench, and he was giving testimony in the Prevezon vs U.S case. You can access his deposition on PACER in the case. So, Browder bankrupts Saturn Investments to avoid paying taxes, and transfers ownership of Dalnaya Steppe to a company named VRMG in Moscow. The new owner, Sashua, and the name of the company, VRMG, are given pseudonyms in his book *Red Notice*. Under video deposition in the Prevezon case, Browder admits he has known Sashua since 1998. Sashua is a security risk manager Browder met through Edmund Safra. His name is spelled different ways, but

I believe pronounced like Sashua. So, through this elaborate layout of companies in Russia and Cyprus, Browder reduced his taxes 35% to 5.5% in Russia and from 15% to 5% in Cyprus. Even his Cyprus companies came under scrutiny because they weren't investing capital in the region but were just "passing through" subsidiaries. Browder ran this tax break "money layering" from 1999-2003 with these two companies, Saturn and Dalnaya Step. The courts interview many of his disabled "employees" and they admit they never even heard of the companies they were working for those four years. In a Moscow Times article covering the corruption case, one of the disabled men, Alexi Bukayev, said he never heard of either Saturn Investment or Dalnaya Step. When he was supposedly working for Magnitsky and Browder, he was working at a bakery and his working papers prove his employment. Another brilliant financial journalist that goes under the name J'Accuse News, has uploaded shortened clips of Browder's Prevezon deposition, making seven, ten minute clips, highlighting parts of the seven hour deposition. He also has uploaded clips from a 2010 documentary titled "Offshore People" and the disabled employees from Browder's shell companies are interviewed under Case #153123. There are several interviews of the disabled employees and he has translated their testimonies. This financial journalist has a way with words and I am just going to copy and paste his description under the video so you get a sense of his mastery of the material and his sharp wit delivering his description of the documentary clip. Adrian also has an excellent website to explore for more information, JAccuse.News.

"Offshore People". Stark. Poetic. The 2010 documentary introduces us to exploited victims of Hermitage enterprise in Kalmykia – for which Bill Browder, American-turned-British agent of deception, is criminally-convicted. Coming soon in English translation @ https://jaccuse.news/page5.html

Before the Magnitsky myth is the reality. In the 1990s, along with the arrival of legitimate operators, predatory capitalists invaded the former Union of Soviet Socialist Republics (USSR 1922 - 1991) on missions pecuniary, political, and/or a mixture of both – "carpet-baggers from the West" in the words of David Cornwell (best known as novelist John le Carré). Among them one William Felix Browder, New Jersey, USA-born (23.04.1964) – a con-man who'd worked for the crooked UK+ 'press baron' Robert Maxwell until the 1991 death of the "Bouncing Czech" off his super-yacht, Lady Ghislaine.

(Maxwell purchased the Lady Ghislaine from the Emad Khashoggi family. Emad's uncle, Saudi arms-dealer Adnan Khashoggi, earned notoriety globally via his association with BCCI – the corrupt Bank of Credit and Commerce International known colloquially as the "Bank of Crooks and Criminals Intl." Adnan made news in Canada in the 1980s when he endeavored to cheat creditors by moving assets through Vancouver Stock Exchange-listed shell companies.)

In the wake of this curious death-at-sea in 1991, ex-Maxwell employee Bill Browder came under the "like gold" wings of a dubious mentor, the Lebanese-Brazilian banker Edmond J. Safra. Safra's Republic National Bank of New York's associated with a number of dodgy Canadian stock deals of the 1980s and '90s – among them: the fraudulent crustacean-trap-to-cellular-privacy share promotion, Cycomm International Inc. (chronicled on earlier pages here); and a mid-'90s mining stock play of Albert Applegath, (the huckster behind New Cinch Uranium Ltd. – Canada's most notorious "salting" or false assaying scandal until gold-fraud Bre-X came along) – more on that deal should time allow. And, not to be left out, Safra's RNBoNY served as Corporate Advisor to Bre-X Minerals Ltd. – the greatest fake-assay swindle in stock market history (cratering in 1997).

As detailed in previous pages on "J'Accuse News" site, for Browder's it's "like winning the lottery" when Edmond Safra (who died, under bizarre circumstances, from smoke-asphyxiation) and French-Israeli "diamond tycoon" Beny Steinmetz, (mired more recently in a massive bribery and money-laundering controversy in Guinea), bank-rolled an operation in Moscow, Hermitage Capital, with him up-front as CEO. Hermitage launched in 1996. (Following Safra's mysterious 1999 demise RNBoNY's sale to HSBC was completed – partnering the latter with Browder's Hermitage team in Russia and offshore, incl. domestic "offshore", locations.)

Encamped in Moscow, in a particularly callous, as well as lucrative scheme, Hermitage group companies for which Bill Browder served as General Director, and Sergei Magnitsky (alt. spellings Sergey, Magnitskiy) acted as Chief Accountant, for years 'employed' disabled people – eg. a victim of the Chernobyl nuclear disaster cleanup, an Afghan war veteran, and one challenged with a genetic disease and mental retardation – claiming them to be expert financial analysts ie. essentially props in a multi-million-dollar tax-fraud. Court found that Browder, Magnitsky and team were "wittingly aware that no work will be performed by the disabled people" and carried out their scheme "without creating jobsites for them". Browder was responsible for filing these sham companies' tax returns – which he duly signed." (End of Excerpt)

Bill Browder's tax accountant, Sergei Magnitsky, who Hermitage hired through the law firm Firestone Duncan, was in charge of obtaining the necessary documents from employees, including the disabled employees who worked for Hermitage. This was confirmed by both Jamie Firestone, founder of law firm Firestone Duncan, and Yulia Chumakova, employee at Firestone Duncan, that helped Magnitsky with the account.

During Browder's video deposition in the Prevezon case he admits his accountants at the time, Arthur Andersen, recommended these tax break set ups, and he insisted he paid the correct taxes and it was all legal. When the case switched from a civil case to a criminal case in Russia, Browder went after Yury Chaika, the lead prosecutor, saying he is part of the "Tsapok Gang". Chaika insisted Browder was smearing him because he didn't want him opening up an investigation into the bankruptcy case in Kalmykia. Chaika's son, Artyom Chaika , was added to the US Magnitsky list, along with twelve other Russian officials, after anti-corruption activist Alexey Navalny released a video that claimed Artyom Chaika was involved in the expropriation of a shipping company in the Far East whose director was allegedly strangled. Clashes between Browder and Chaika would continue to make headlines over the next decade, as both would go back and forth accusing each other of crimes. Alexey Navalny, a Russian human rights activist, and former politician would frequently team up with Bill Browder and Western Putin critics to accuse Chaika of corruption. The punk rock band, Pussy Riot, piled on to these accusations and put out a satirical music video titled "Chaika". The four women group was heavily promoted by Bill Browder, and he even brought them to Capitol Hill. Their "activism", which includes disgusting antics in art museums, churches and grocery stores, is not mentioned by Browder, and you will just have to Google it because I don't have the stomach to write it out or footnote.

Browder's back and forths to Moscow came to a dramatic stop in 2005 when he says he was not allowed to leave the airport when he landed in Russia. After a long arduous detainment sorting out the details, he was placed on an airplane to London, never to step foot on Russia soil again. This is the scenario Browder describes in his book, so it's unclear of what the exact circumstances are at this point. I have a hard time believing anything that comes out of this man's mouth. The way he can recollect the tiniest detail in his storytelling in Red Notice down to the color of a man's shirt, but under video deposition he says

"I don't know" to so many questions is alarming. For him to answer, "I don't remember" to the question "Does anyone, including yourself, attempt to contact Magnitsky or Magnitsky's lawyers?" is just an answer I will never forget. This is the man who has spent the last decade spreading his story to the world, but an eleven-month detention in prison, with, according to Browder, daily torture, and there were no attempts at communicating with Magnitsky's lawyers? In fact, it gets worse than that as I recently read in a new *Der Spiegel* article that has a great exposé on Browder. The article by Benjamin Bidder states a human rights advocate who worked with Mikhail Khodorkovsky, who frequently visited the prisoners, was never even made aware of Magnitsky's detention. I mean, this would be the first person Browder would contact to find out anything about Sergei, but she was never contacted. The first time Zoya Svetova ever heard of Sergei was when she read about his death in the newspaper. She went over to the prison right away, and within days, wrote extensively about her interviews with staff and fellow prisoners. At that point no one was suspecting violence, only the medical care around the circumstances of his death.

Chapter 7

FRAMING RUSSIAN COPS

DER SPIEGEL IS the first prominent newspaper in any country to really shine a light on Browder's manipulation framing the Sergei Magnitsky story. The author, Benjamin Bidder, highlights Zoya Svetova's initial human rights report and other human rights reports on Magnitsky's death. I highly recommend reading the *Der Spiegel* article. Browder calls the whole article Russian disinformation and Benjamin Bidder doesn't back down to Browder's smears. Benjamin responds to Browder's complaints with an even more scathing article than the original. He includes multiple links to open sources, including many of Zoya Svetova's interviews right after Magnitsky's death.

So, now we have Browder kicked out of Russia and his Hermitage Fund employees and Firestone Duncan employees still living in the country. Browder says he makes requests to reenter the country, even speaking directly to Prime Minister Medvedev in Davos to help him but is unsuccessful. The case against Browder and Magnitsky continues on and Sergei Magnitsky is brought in for questioning in 2006 for case #248065. Now bear in mind this 2006 testimony is well before the 2007 Russian treasury theft that occurred, but Browder insists the Kalmykia investigation into him and Magnitsky had closed at this point. I know this gets confusing as there are a lot of courts, companies, and lawyers, but just to make it clear, this 2006 testimony is before the 2007 theft that Browder claims Magnitsky was the whistleblower to. I recommend everyone read this 2006 testimony as Sergei admits he hadn't even spoken to Browder for over three years, so this would mean, in 2006, they had no communication during the years 2003-2006. Remember, Magnitsky has worked for Firestone Duncan since the late 90s, so he was familiar with Bill Browder since the late 90s.

This 2006 police testimony is labelled Case #248065 and it's clearly in regard to Magnitsky's involvement in the Hermitage companies in Kalmykia. Magnitsky admits in the 2006 questioning he is probably the CEO of Saturn Investments and admits his signature is on the paperwork confirming he was a founder of the company. This testimony was submitted as evidence in the Prevezon case in New York and Browder was asked questions about the signed testimony, admitting it was probably Magnitsky's signature on the paper. Browder insists an investigation opened in 2004 and closed in 2005 in regard to Saturn and Dalnaya Steppe, so he is unsure about the origins of the document. He may be correct on that, but it is clear from Magnitsky's 2006 testimony, the questions are related to Magnitsky and Saturn Investment. Browder says the crooked cops, Kuznetsov and Karpov, stole the companies and money, and Sergei was the whistleblower to their crimes. Why is Magnitsky "blowing the whistle" in 2006 on a crime that happens in 2007? This makes no sense. Browder deliberately just mashes all three of his criminal investigations into one big plot against him, but if you break it down, you realize it is three separate cases. Magnitsky's testimony and other court documents certainly don't back up any of Browder's claims. Just to make sure you are following along; we had a 2004 investigation into Browder and Magnitsky's tax fraud in Kalmykia with the companies Saturn and Dalnaya Step. Later there will be a court case where they are found guilty of crimes with these two companies. In 2006 Magnitsky is brought to the police for questioning about his name on the ownership of the Saturn Investment company, Case #248065. Then, Browder's offices are raided with a warrant for questionable corruption in another company named "Kameya". This gets confusing because it's a separate company, separate corruption case from Saturn Investment and Dalnaya Step and the disabled "employees". Steppe is the topographical description of the region in Russia where the city of Kalmykia is located, so I remember those companies with the Steppe spelling association. Confused? Probably. Me too. Let's drop the criminal investigation on Saturn and Dalnaya Step for now. The second case, the Kameya case, is the reason for the warrant, and the third case is the one Browder's whole story is about, the "stolen" companies. But, were they stolen? The police are trying to figure it all out with questioning Magnitsky to see if he was part of the scam of "stealing" companies he represents. Magnitsky is brought in for questioning to the police in 2007 in regard to his knowledge and participation in giving a Hermitage lawyer powers of attorney. Eduard Khairetdinov' name is on the paperwork for the arbitration hearings of the so called "stolen companies". This guy Eduard Khairetdinov is an important name to remember in this mystery. Remember, tall, mustache, "alibi" guy. *The Magnitsky Act* film director outlines Magnitsky's sit downs with the police on his website MagnitskyAct.com. Of Magnitsky's numerous police summons, Browder only mentions those on June 5, 2008, and October 7th, 2008, but refers to them as whistleblower "testimonies". He makes no references to the sit downs with the police in 2007 before and after the May and June 2007 police raids when the police allegedly "stole" the seals.

So the raid on Hermitage is for a warrant on the "Kameya" case. Later, a case opens up about the $230 million Russian treasury theft that involves the R/P/M companies. Three crimes with different companies in each case, but all initially owned by Browder's company Hermitage. I will label these companies as R/P/M, for Rilend/Parfenion/Makhaon. Think of RPM, as in revolutions per minute to help keep track. I like to use a lot of word association for all these Russian names. For these Hermitage companies, think of a three-tiered pyramid. The bottom of the pyramid are these three shell companies, R/P/M, which are in Moscow. Their directors are in the middle of the pyramid, Glendora and Kone, and those shell companies are in Cyprus. The top of the pyramid is HSBC and they are located on the Island of Guernsey off the coast of France. The top and the middle have powers of attorney over the bottom of the pyramid. This is the legitimate set up. No one is denying this is how Browder set up his companies. See why they call it money layering? I haven't even mentioned the "stolen companies" yet, that's a second pyramid. In Browder's book about the raids on Hermitage Capital and Firestone Duncan, there is very dramatic scene, with one of Firestone Duncan's employees getting beaten up during the raid and has to go to the hospital. I have listened to Jamie Firestone in speeches online explaining how this employee was hospitalized for two weeks. Other times he has said he was hospitalized for three months. The details are a bit murky about this employee and he is given a pseudonym in all articles, so tough to research. On Browder's website, there is a description of the incident with a picture of a 1960s hospitalized patient in the hospital bed with facial injuries. This picture is of a Famous *Freedom Rider* from the United States, so this doesn't help. Browder would do many power point presentations using WordArt and pictures to make a story easy for people to follow. During the raids on Hermitage and Firestone Duncan, the police seize computers, documents, and corporate seals of Browder's companies. Browder says a Firestone Duncan employee refused to open up a safe containing documents and that is why he was fined rubles and beaten up. This story doesn't make sense to me. The Russian cops beat the guy so bad he has to be in the hospital for three months, and then they fine him on top of that? The corporate seals of the companies R/P/M

(Rilend, Parfenion, and Makhaon) were taken during the raid as well as documents about the Kameya company. In Andrei Nekrasov' film, he uses dramatic scenes of the raid with Kuznetsov looking menacing and intimidating the employees. In reality, the lead police officer was a woman who did the raid on Hermitage Capital, and she was not in full riot gear. Now the crooks have the paperwork for the bottom of the pyramid, and also the crooks supposedly have powers of attorney over the middle of the pyramid. They change the name of the middle of the three-tiered pyramid from Glendora and Kone in Cyprus to Pluto in Kazan, Tatarstan, and the top of the pyramid is changed from HSBC in Guernsey Island to Boily Systems in British Virgin Islands. This is easy to visualize. Just take the first pyramid and replace with the second pyramid. Identical three-tiered pyramids with just different names in each section. Andrei stated on his website, **"Browder emphasized everybody was corrupt but him. "Browder describes the post-Soviet privatization as a "win-win situation": The state gave away all "the shares of all the companies to the people for free. Everyone could have made a lot of money out of it". When he personally experienced difficulties with Russian tax investigators and could no longer make bumper profits, good Russian capitalism suddenly came to an end. Since then, according to Browder, an era of complete corruption and human rights violations has dawned in Russia."**

Andrei goes on to say in his article; **'For most Russians, the rush for communist property was a kind of "controlled civil war" overseen by the IMF, the "Chicago Boys" from Harvard, Goldman Sachs and others. The majority of the population was the loser. Magnitsky was certainly the victim of unforgivable medical negligence and the Russian penal system, but he also fell victim to the post-Soviet gold rush of privatization, which enriched Browder and his foreign investors.**

Browder and his helpers skillfully control the Magnitsky narrative with PowerPoint presentations, which they regularly adapt to the course of events and spread among the allies and the unsuspecting public through various channels. The unhinged use of Browder's private press releases as relentlessly efficient political combat weaponry, says a lot about the corporate media spreading unverified, copy pasted information." (End of Nekrasov quote)

After the raids, Hermitage Capital puts together a series of videos they uploaded to YouTube to describe what happened to them in Russia. One of the videos, *"Law and Order"*, was played the last ten minutes of Browder's Stanford Business school speech. The last thirty seconds talks about Sergei's arrest.

The warrant for the May 28th, 2007 police raid was for charges that his company Kameya took profits out of country and owed 50,000,000 rubles in taxes. In the Hermitage company video *"Law and Order the Hermitage story"*, Browder states the police claimed the company Kameya withheld dividend taxes but Browder states he has a document that shows he overpaid. During 2015 Prevezon deposition case he promised he would produce this document at the next deposition, which never occurred. A week later, June 4th, 2007, Kuznetsov ordered a raid on Hermitage Capital and the same day Firestone Duncan was raided. As mentioned earlier, a young lawyer, who protested the raid was allegedly beaten, fined 15,000 rubles, and needed to be hospitalized from injuries.

Browder then makes the claim in the *"Law and Order"* YouTube video that Kuznetsov went to the Russian courts in Kazan, St Petersburg, and Moscow and obtained judgements on the basis of forged contracts using the corporate seals he confiscated in the raids. He and his "Klyuev Gang" used real people representing Hermitage in court, Yulia Mayorova, Ekaterina Maltzeva, and Andrei Pavlov. Instead of defending Hermitage, they pled guilty, awarding the companies R/P/M hundreds of millions of dollars. The stolen companies were then put under criminals' names that were recently released from prison. Now, the criminals were the recipients of the tax rebate scam to cheat the Russian treasury out of $230 million. The set up for the fraud was Hermitage was 1.2 billion in debt and was entitled to $230 million in tax refund from the government. Browder claims the only way the crooks could have stolen the companies was with the original seals and certificates used during the raids. (I believe all this is true, but just replace Kuznetsov with Browder and Magnitsky, and "original seals" with "duplicate seals" and that's what may have happened.) Browder claims initially the plan was for Kuznetsov to go to the banks to steal the assets of Hermitage that were in accounts at HSBC, Citibank, ING, CreditSuisse but he would discover there were no assets in the banks as Browder pulled out all Hermitage assets the year before. So after they discovered there were no assets, they went to plan B, which was the tax refund fraud stealing from the Russian treasury. Browder claims on December 24th, 2007, the crooks put in a tax rebate claim and got $230 million. On one video, the narrator specifically names Olga Tzymai and Sergei Zemchuznikov of the Moscow tax bureau, granted the tax rebate the next day. The $230 million was deposited into two obscure banks. They laundered the money and liquidated the stolen Hermitage companies. Hermitage filed dozens of complaints and no one on the anti-corruption team of the President Medvedev helped Hermitage. Throughout the video the narrator is using a very menacing voice and the music adds to the confirmation that Karpov and Kuznetsov are really really bad guys. *The HermitageTV* YouTube channel has a playlist of a lot of the "Untouchable" videos, as well as other interviews Browder has done over the years.

We have to remember that at this time in Russia, there is a lot of rampant corruption going on unchecked. The basic scam, to get your taxes back from the Federal government, had occurred in many companies, with some legitimate theft of companies, and others pretending their companies were stolen. The scam went like this: We had a contract and you didn't fill it, so we are suing you. This is what happened in the Hermitage case. An unknown contractor sued Hermitage for a certain amount of money and the fake Hermitage employees in court admit they didn't pay the contractor and so the judge says, "Hermitage needs to pay the contractor". So now, because Hermitage had to pay out this big fine, their taxes are off because they overpaid, not anticipating this "great loss" from having to pay a contractor back. So, they request a tax refund, because they paid too much taxes and the tax offices grant them this refund. They have successfully stolen from the Russian treasury.

This type of tax fraud occurred with the investment company, Renaissance Capital, in 2006, the year before the tax fraud with the Hermitage companies. Renaissance claims the 107-million-dollar fraud happened after they sold their companies to a subsidiary and they were innocent. Browder has made claims that RenCap (Renaissance Capital) was behind the Hermitage tax fraud as well because the same players were involved; Andrei Pavlov, Dmitry Klyuev, and even the same tax officers. Michael Weiss of *The Daily Beast* and the Organization OCCRP, write about how RenCap (Renaissance Capital) was behind the Hermitage heist with "The Klyuev Gang".

Prior to the tax heist, Hermitage knew that their companies were stolen and they filed detailed complaints December 3rd and December 6th, 2007 about their companies being stolen. When the film director Andrei Nekrasov asked one of the Hermitage employees about these complaints, he described them as an "alibi". Nekrasov thought this was an odd term to use. Andrei finds the receipt of their complaints and shows a close up of the document in his documentary and it looks like the date was altered. This could mean that they didn't even complain about the companies stolen at the beginning of December but may have back dated to that date. Andrei at this point in the film, seems open to a reasonable explanation to these changes on a document, and I think if Browder was truthful, he could have given Andrei an explanation. Another document Nekrasov shows is their complaint doesn't even mention the companies' names that were supposedly stolen or an address. The English translation says millions of Browder's assets were stolen, even though he says he had no assets in Russia at the time. At this point in trying to piece together his documentary, *The Magnitsky Act,* Andrei Nekrasov could not get Browder on the phone. Nekrasov has to confront the Hermitage employees at the New York book launch of Browder's book *Red Notice*. Browder was quick to brush him off. The employee who said the complaints were an "alibi", was Eduard Khairetdinov, a tall lawyer in the firm with a mustache that Magnitsky's testimony was based on. The case was # 374015, concerning the issuance of the Powers of Attorney to Mr. E.M Khairetdinov. The Russian cops were asking Magnitsky why he helped give Khairetdinov powers of attorney to supposedly "stolen" companies. Andrei Nekrasov again tries to get Browder's attention in London, when Browder was leaving a libel court case brought against him by one of the Russian cops, Karpov. Browder was quick to brush him off again, giving a brief statement outside the courtroom before walking away from the director. After the brazen 2007 December tax return heist, 2008 rolls in, and on April 3rd, 2008, another criminal investigation of Browder opens up as first reported by *The Financial Times* with Moscow reporter, Catherine Belton. Browder has been out of the country for over two years, but now, he and another Hermitage employee are being investigated for a criminal tax violation. According to The Financial Times article on April 5th, 2008, the Moscow interior ministry launched a criminal tax probe last June 2007 into a company linked to Hermitage, which Mr. Browder has stated is groundless.

On April 7th, 2008 an article called, *"Hijacking the Hermitage Fund"*, popped up on Hermitage website discussing the stolen companies.

On April 9th, 2008, a woman who was the figurehead to the three shell companies 000 R/P/M, had read about the charges brought against Browder and went to the police station in Kazan to give a statement on her knowledge of the companies she oversaw. She was nervous to be implicated in the crime. She may have gotten scared because of enormity of the amount of money being discussed. Rimma Starova was the figurehead used in the $230 million tax rebate fraud and served as Chief Executive of 000 Rilend, 000 Parfenion, and 000 Makhaon, Browder's three companies. She was a hired to front the liquidation of these companies. She read about Browder's charges in the Russian newspaper *Kommersant*. Her police testimony is key to understanding *" the biggest treasury theft in Russian history"*. She is the whistleblower in this case, not Sergei Magnitsky who was being questioned by police.

June 5th, 2008. Magnitsky is brought in for questioning.

July 24th, 2008. a NYT article comes out describing the tax fraud.

September 2008. Another Russian newspaper, *Vedomosti,* talks about the tax fraud as well.

September 2008. Hermitage website talks about $230 million stolen from Russian treasury.

October 7th, 2008. Sergei is brought in again for questioning. Browder insists this October testimony is when Magnitsky blows the whistle on Karpov and Kuznetsov, but they are not even named in this police testimony. He mentions them in June testimony, but doesn't say they were involved in the fraud, just that they confiscated the seals of Hermitage.

November 2008. Sergei is arrested but didn't give any declaration accusing Karpov and Kuznetsov of the tax refund fraud. There is no sentence in any of his police testimony accusing Karpov and Kuznetsov of the treasury theft. (That statement doesn't come until October 2009, one month before he died.)

March 2009. Rimma Starova's whistleblowing story disappears from the Hermitage website.

Framing Russian Cops

March 2009. Sergei the whistleblower story emerges for the first time, four months after his death.

The rest of this chapter is details on the criminals who stole the companies. Just skip to the next chapter if you don't want your head to spin.

March 2009. Hermitage begins to file claims to the Arbitration court to get control of their companies back, Glendora Holding and 000 Parfenion, specifically in one case. (Glendora and 000 Parfenion were supposedly stolen but the courts say you never claim they are stolen in your complaint! Hermitage was just asking the courts to change the name back but never says the "bad guy" stole the companies. Why?)

So, to keep track, just remember Browder is accusing the bad guys of stealing his companies (Rilend, Parfenion, and Makhaon), and renaming 000 Rilend, 000 Parfenion, and 000 Makhaon. The new bad guy owners are Kurochkin, Khlebnikov, and Markelov. They make another bad guy in charge, named Gasanov. Gasanov is supposed to be the super bad guy that is now in charge of telling the other bad guys what to do. Gasanov is supposed to be in charge of Glendora illegally (The middle of the second pyramid).

Glendora and Kone Holdings would continue to have ownership of 000 Parfenion. This makes you ask the question, if the courts say the powers of attorney were real (Hermitage knowingly gave Gasanov power of attorney), did the criminals act with Browder's knowledge and interest? To summarize the bad guys. Bad guy Gasanov gets power of attorney to give other bad guys Markelov, Kurochkin, and Khlebnikov permission to steal the money. When Browder tries to take the bad guys names off the companies, the courts say why? You show no proof the companies were stolen! So, Browder drops the case. It would be interesting to ask all these questions to Gasanov, but he is dead. Valery Kurochkin is dead too. Markelov is still alive after serving five years for his role in the Russian treasury theft, but he has not been available for interviews. Khlebnikov is still alive and he, Browder, and Markelov, are facing new charges just issued by The Russian Federation for the Russian Treasury theft. Lucy Komisar spoke about these charges in a September 2019 interview on the podcast *"Around the Empire"* and Lucy stated she knows Browder is taking it seriously because he has petitioned the Federal Court in the Southern District of New York to subpoena bank records from J.P. Morgan bank. He has stated some U.S banks have some of the $230 million stolen Russian treasury money. This is an attempt to "go on the offense" against these new charges.

Gasanov is the middleman who mysteriously dies once the transfer of the ownership of the three Hermitage companies was completed to Markelov, Khlebnikov, and Kurochkin. No proof of murder of Gasanov and Kurochkin, but they are both now dead. Also, in Nekrasov' documentary, he mentions the owner of the bank, Sergei Korobeinikov (which a portion of the stolen Russian treasury money was wired), fell out of a window and died, so there's that.

When Markelov was questioned by the police, he named Khairetdinov and Vadim Kleiner as involved in the re registering of the companies. Both Eduard Khairetdinov and Vadim Kleiner are employees of Hermitage Capital. Markelov also claimed to see Gasanov with "Sergei Leonidovich". Magnitsky's name is typed Sergei Leonidovich Magnitsky in most legal documents.

So, the search for who is behind the Russian stolen treasury money goes on, but with Browder's conviction in the Saturn Investment and Dalnaya Steppe case, his conviction in the Kameya case, and now new charges against Browder into the Russian treasury theft case, Russia is determined to investigate Browder.

Chapter 8

MAGNITSKY'S YEAR IN JAIL AND DEATH

SERGEI WAS ARRESTED in November 2008 and was placed in pre-trial detention awaiting his case for charges of tax evasion in Kalmykia with the disabled employee companies. He had health problems while he was in prison and spent a month in the medical wing of Butyrka prison before he transferred to Matrosskaya Tishina on Monday, November 16th, 2009. The day he died. During his detention, he developed and was diagnosed with cholelithiasis and chronic active cholecystopancreatitis. Browder claims in letters to the authorities and his family, "Sergei complained about his treatment more than 450 times during the time he was detained", although these were never made public. The only handwritten notes of complaints made public were 25 handwritten by Magnitsky and filed by Butyrka prison between July 26th, 2009 and September 2009. Among these handwritten notes are statements where he states he wasn't treated more harshly than the other prisoners the first ten months, and the doctors treated him adequately.

At Butyrka prison Sergei was seen by doctors when he had complaints, but no documentations of any life-threatening conditions. He was seen by the doctor on the Friday before he died and the doctor said she would check on Sergei on Monday. On that Monday, the day of his death, November 16, 2009, Magnitsky complained of pain and vomiting, and was transferred from the detention center FBU IZ 77/2 of UFSIN (Butyrka) to the hospital of FBU IZ 77/1 (Matrosskaya Tishina) of the Russian Corrective Service (UFSIN). The doctor decided to transfer him from Butykra prison to Matrosskaya prison so he could get an ultrasound and work up for possible surgery. When she called Matrosskaya prison explaining the patient had pancreatitis, the doctor on the other side of the phone asked if it was acute and she said, 'no', and he then asked, "then why the hell did he need to come to their prison?" CCTV (Closed circuit TV) shows Sergei carrying his three bags and a couple of plastic bags to the transport ambulance to Matrosskaya prison. There is some confusion if the CCTV at Matrosskaya shows him walking into the prison in the same condition as when he left Butyrka, but eyewitnesses said he did walk into the prison and there is some video of him walking in, but a camera only catches his back.

There, he was evaluated for his symptoms, thought to be cholecystitis and pancreatitis. At this time, between approximately 6:20pm and 7:30pm, Magnitsky exhibited behavior diagnosed as "acute psychosis" by Dr. A. V. Gaus, at which point the doctor ordered Mr. Magnitsky to be restrained with handcuffs. At 7:30pm Gaus called for an emergency psychiatric team to evaluate and treat Mr. Magnitsky. Dr. Gaus did not return to Mr. Magnitsky until 9:20pm, at which time the patient was unconscious. Gaus then ordered his transfer to the intensive care ward, where resuscitation measures were taken. Mr. Magnitsky was pronounced dead at 9:50pm by Gaus. According to statements made by members of the Psychiatric First-Aid Mobile Team of Moscow, they received a request to attend to a patient at FBU IZ

77/1 of UFSIN at 7:40pm on November 16, 2009. They arrived at the location at 8:00pm, but were not admitted into the detention facility until approximately 9:00pm. Contrary to Gaus' statement, the first-aid team says they found the victim in a regular jail cell, rather than the medical ward (as per testimonies by Kornilov and Morozov in the 12 May 2010 report). The psychiatrists confirmed his death to have occurred between approximately 9:00 and 9:15pm. According to the autopsy report and a subsequent investigation conducted by a Medical Commission between February 2, 2010 and May 12, 2010, the cause of death was attributed to acute heart failure with dilated cardiomyopathy. The Medical Commission's report stated: "At the moment of his death, S.L. Magnitsky had no aggravations of cholelithiasis or pancreatitis (peritonitis, pancreatic abscess, ulcers, decubital ulcers of gall bladder with perforation and hemorrhage, stomach wall and transverse colon necrosis, gastrointestinal hemorrhage and others), individually the specified diseases have no relation to the occurrence of death." On a preliminary report a doctor wrote 'closed cerebral injury?', but this remark did not make it into the final report. I think they put in the preliminary report based on his psychotic behavior the three hours in their care and perhaps wanted to rule out previous head trauma from his chart. Once they saw no past medical history of traumatic brain injury, this did not make it into the final report. The glaring contradictions between Dr Gaus and the psychiatric team on the location of Magnitsky's body is a big red flag, as Dr Gaus says they transferred him to the intensive care ward and the psychiatric team states Sergei was in a regular ward cell. These types of contradictions complicate an investigation, especially one when an accusation of murder is on the line. What further complicates this alleged murder is an international law is named after this man. So, was Sergei a crooked accountant justly imprisoned for his crimes, who because of his poor health and poor conditions in prison, died a premature death? Was he a brave whistleblower who uncovered a crime and went to the police as a whistleblower and then was murdered because he knew too much? In Browder's book he writes, "Sergei demanded that the lead officer call his lawyer and the prosecutor. Sergei said, 'I'm here because I've exposed the five-point-four billion rubles that were stolen by law enforcement officers.' But the riot guards weren't there to help him, they were there to beat him. And they laid into him viciously with their rubber batons. One hour and eighteen minutes later, a civilian doctor arrived and found Sergei Magnitsky dead on the floor." How does Browder know Sergei says this? I mean, seriously, can anyone explain how Browder knows this? What is the name of the witness that gave Browder this quote? It is nowhere in any of the human rights reports after his death. I will link the *Public Oversight Committee Moscow* report and the *Physicians for Human Rights Report* out of Cambridge, MA that clearly contradict many details in the book *Red Notice* about the circumstances surrounding his death. Are these contradictions minor details that are insignificant to the larger symbolic gesture of the Magnitsky Act? Some of the contradictions Browder states are that Magnitsky had to sleep in a cell with a broken window in December where he nearly froze to death, but the Public Oversight Committee Moscow showed the window was broken in September. Browder states Magnitsky had to stay in a cell without enough cots, so they had to take turns sleeping, but again, according to the POC report there is no report of a cell without enough cots.

Cell 206 (12 beds, 10 inmates, 48.2 square meters) - Cell 309 (8 beds, 7 inmates, 32.1 square meters) - Cell 417(14 beds, 12 inmates, 56.2 square meters) - Cell 503 (9 beds, 8 inmates, 36.4 square meters) 8 bed, 7 inmates, 14 bed, 12 inmates, and 9 bed, 8 inmates, so there were actually always extra beds in the documentation.

Browder will also describe how Magnitsky had to live in conditions where the floor in the ground that was the toilet would bubble up so he had to live amongst raw sewage on the floor, but again, the *Public Oversight Committee* in Moscow showed he only had to live with a broken toilet for less than 36 hours.

Cell 35 (from September 8 to 10, 2009). The living space here is 10.1 square meters. There are 6 beds, and there were three inmates in it. The cell windows had no glass in them; the walls of the cell were wet. On Magnitsky's second day in this cell, raw sewage under the toilet began to rise, and by evening sewage water covered half of the cell. The inmates asked that the problem be fixed, the plumber did not come until 10 p.m., and he was not able to fix the problem. The inmates asked to be moved to another cell, but they were left in the cell till morning. The next day, the plumber did not come, and the sewage water continued to flood the entire cell floor. The inmates moved around the cell by walking on beds. The plumber only came in the evening, he was trying to fix the trouble for a long time, but he failed. Both the plumber and the warden who brought the plumber were expressing indignation over the conditions in which the inmates had to live. They were asked to move the inmates to another cell, but those employees were not in a position to decide on their transfer without their superiors' approval. The permission was only received at 11 p.m., after which the inmates were moved to Cell 61. Magnitsky and his fellow inmates had lived in the midst of raw sewage for 35 hours.

Now, I am by no means minimizing the harsh and inhumane conditions that Magnitsky was subjected to while being incarcerated. It appeared these prisons were hell, but why the need to exaggerate or change the details of the Human Rights reports if they show neglect and poor conditions? They are harsh enough without the need to alter the facts. Did the story not sound packaged enough for a fifteen-minute TED talk? I would like to ask Browder, but he protects himself from any questions.

Zoya Svetova, a member of the *Public Oversight Committee Moscow*, was exposing the numerous violations of rules and regulations when she visited the prison frequently as an advocate for prison rights. Zoya, as I stated earlier, knew nothing about Sergei Magnitsky and was never asked to check on him or advocate for him. No one from Hermitage ever made her aware of his incarceration. So, what was the point of all those complaints Magnitsky wrote that Browder states he was receiving? How was Browder receiving these documents during Sergei's detention if Browder "doesn't remember" interacting with Magnitsky's lawyers? Why had no one filed any complaints to any human rights advocacy group anywhere throughout his eleven-month pretrial detention? Browder even spoke to the *Congressional Human Rights Committee* in Washington D.C, organized by a Massachusetts representative and co-chair of the committee a month before Magnitsky died. Browder spoke about his ill treatment by Russia. Not his Russian lawyer's ill treatment, but Browder's ill treatment. Was Sergei beaten? We know there are multiple discrepancies in the reports filed to Congress and media compared to the original documents. The original report states the restraints used on Sergei during his detention had been written "special means were" but it was replaced by "a rubber baton was". 'Special means' in this circumstance means that Sergei was handcuffed. It did not mean rubber baton. If you read further in the report it states that the handcuffs were applied because the medical staff were concerned about the patient self-harming himself. Once the patient calmed down, the handcuffs were removed and patient was not checked on for an hour and eighteen minutes.

Some of the testimony of the employees of Matrosskaya stated the reason that Magnitsky had special means applied to him was because he was experiencing acute psychosis and they were concerned for his safety. Major Dmitry F. Markov, Aid to Head of Detention Center on Duty (DPNSI), discussed the events around the restraining of Magnitsky. (DPNSI is the abbreviation for the prison guards).

He was one of the most senior officers on duty at Matrosskaya Tishina detention center, and he was involved in the application of special means to restrain Mr. Magnitsky before his death and the subsequent "cover up". This second forged document replaces "special means applied" with "used a rubber baton". Read the forged statement below with the words "used a rubber baton" added and read again with the original words "special means applied". Which makes more sense to you? Browder's version submitted to the United States Congress reads Markov wrote, "Act on the use of handcuffs. 16.11.2009 at 18 hr 30 min. Deputy Aid to Head of Detention Center on Duty O.G Kuznetsov at the post of collection unit in accordance with Article 45 of the Law on Detention....and Article 30 Penal Bodies "used a rubber baton" in relation to suspect, accused, Magnitsky Sergei Leonidovich. Handcuffs were used due to a threat to commit an act of bodily harm and suicide. The handcuffs were taken off at 20 hr 00min on 16.11.2009." Now, if you just read this paragraph and compare it to the original report that stated "special needs applied" and read it a couple of time with each phrase, "used a rubber baton" vs "special needs applied", to me, it seems obvious the natural flow of the sentence structure makes sense with the words, "special needs applied". Here, read how it sounded before the forgery. "Act on the use of handcuffs. 16.11.2009 at 18 hr 30 min. Deputy Aid to Head of Detention Center on Duty O.G Kuznetsov at the post of collection unit in accordance with Article 45 of the Law on Detention....and Article 30 Penal Bodies "special means applied" in relation to suspect, accused, Magnitsky Sergei Leonidovich. Handcuffs were used due to a threat to commit an act of bodily harm and suicide. The handcuffs were taken off at 20 hr 00min on 16.11.2009." Did Browder forge the documents he submitted to the United Stated Congress when lobbying for the Magnitsky Act? We know he was accused of forging documents in the Kalmykia case and submitted forged documents of the Public Oversight Report to the WSJ, and now another forgery discovery to Congress. Is this the third time he was caught forging a document? There are other examples of questionable forgery we can discuss later as well.

To continue some of the other witness testimonies surrounding the death of Sergei:

G.V Kharlamov examined Magnitsky's body after his death and he stated, "no signs of violent death were found".

Alexander Kuleshov was a senior officer responsible for the health and life of Mr. Magnitsky and he noted that "his forehead was sweating, the face was very pale, the eyes were expanded." States he "stayed at the collection unit until Magnitsky calmed down and then left the collection unit. 15-20 minutes later a man on duty called me and said S.L. Magnitsky felt poorly again and emergency ambulance was called".

Dr Gaus is probably the most significant eyewitness to the last hours of Sergei's life as she was the doctor on duty and co-signed the act of death of Sergei. Dr Gaus states she "**saw Magnitsky in the nurse's cabinet. He was accompanied by the guard from Butyrka, and he was already in a special isolation cell. As it was mentioned earlier, the transfer documents were delivered by the young nurse from the ambulance. Magnitsky said that he had been sick since Thursday, November 12th, when he started feeling abdominal pains. During the survey, his abdomen was tense; he felt pains in both left and right parts of the area which is an obvious symptom of pancreatitis. In the medical records, she read prescription to a repeat ultrasound examination. During the survey, Magnitsky had twice a desire to vomit (with no vomiting) and she gave him a hygienic bag. Initially he was calm, agreed to a hospitalization and signed on the medical records. At 19:00 suddenly he started behaving anxiously, started to talk: "Why are you inspecting my bags?" He had three bags and two plastic bags. She replied "Nobody is inspecting your bags." He: "No, you see that they are being inspected now!" And seized the metal bar on the bench that was in the isolation cell where he was during questioning. (Afterwards we observed that it would be hard to swing the bench inside the cell due to the cell's small size) He then sat down and covered himself with a plastic bag and said that they want to kill him. It continued for a short period of time and he hit twice the floor with the cot, then put it back and scared** and started to hide behind the plastic bag again, which she gave to him. According to her opinion it looked like acute psychosis and delirium of persecution. They called for psychiatric emergency... medical assistant Sash made the injection under her prescription and came to surgery. She didn't see psychiatrists. At 21:20 a female voice called from entrance department and informed that a patient is on the floor in the 4th isolation cell.

Medical conditions are questionable. The doctor on duty, Nafikov, ran in to perform resuscitation procedures with the help of special equipment (cushion of Ambu)". When Dr Gaus was asked about restraints she said "....called enforcement DPNSI Fedorovich (Dmitry Fedorovich Markov) who came with approximately eight people. They put handcuffs on Magnitsky's hand. He didn't oppose them, but stayed in handcuffs, looked inadequate and gazed around."

As Doctor on duty, she co-signed the act of death of Mr Magnitsky. She wrote **"Act of Death....we state the death of: Magnitsky Sergei Leonidovich born 1972 occurring on 16 November 2009 at 21 hr 50 min (9:50 p.m).**

Cause of death: Toxic shock. Acute cardio-vascular insufficiency.

Diagnosis: Gallstone: Acute calculous cholesystitis. Acute pancreatitis. Pancreonecrosis? Acute psychosis. Closed cerebral trauma? (End of Dr Gaus' testimony)

The *Physicians for Human Rights (PHR)* group in Cambridge, MA looked at the Moscow Human rights report, plus dozens of documents submitted to them by Bill Browder. They write about a "piercing" on the tongue of Magnitsky. The PHR looked at many documents investigating the case, including the Forensic Medical Examination Office report. Report by Forensic Medical Examination Office team May 12, 2010, stated 'The puncture wound at the root of the tongue documented during the victim's autopsy was reported as attempts to resuscitate him. Therefore, no reason existed for chemical forensic examinations of this area. This report was written by A.N. Borzova, December 31st, 2009, and includes the tongue description in 1 of 9 of its findings on the autopsy. In 2015 testimony in the Prevezon case, head of the human rights report in Moscow, Kirill Kabanov, repudiated Browder's evidence of a beating. Judge Pauley agreed with Kabanov' testimony based on a ruling in Council of Europe report and said Browder's evidence was inadmissible.

The Physicians for Human Rights finding on review of available case documents stated "The puncture wound noted to the tongue should have been removed" (the tongue) "and submitted for toxicological examination. This was not done according to the autopsy protocol and no toxicological testing was performed by the Minnesota Protocol."

Dr Alexandra Gaus was put on trial, accused of negligence in the death of Sergei Magnitsky and was put through a lot of emotional and financial hardship defending herself. Of course any doctor is going to be upset when a patient dies under their care, and I'm sure if she could have saved his life or done something different that night she would turn back time. Working in a prison is a difficult job, and I have sympathy for Dr Gaus and her staff.

Dr Gaus and three other prison doctors were placed on the sanctions list written up by Senator Ben Cardin, for withholding proper medical care to Sergei while he was being held in pretrial detention. Dr Larisa Litinova charges were dropped on April 9th, 2012 due to statute of limitations issues. Four of the twelve placed on the sanctions list were doctors. (60 people were originally proposed by Bill Browder.) This patient was only in their care for about three hours before he died. CCTV shows he walked into the transport vehicle from Butykra prison carrying his bags and eyewitnesses say he walked into Matrosskaya

Tishina prison from the vehicle.

Dr Kratov, one of the doctors sanctioned by the United States, was charged in Russia court system, but on December 23, 2012, as the trial neared its end, the prosecutor conducting the trial against Dr Kratov suddenly reversed course and sought acquittal. The judge cited no direct connection between Kratov' actions and Magnitsky's death. On December 28th, 2012, a Tverskoy court found Kratov not guilty of negligence causing Magnitsky's death, thus complying with the prosecution's request.

What is strange here is Dmitry F. Markov, one of the riot guards who is supposedly admitted he used a rubber baton in restraining Magnitsky, (really probably forged paperwork with replacing original "special means applied" to "used a rubber baton") isn't put on Ben Cardin's list of human rights abusers. There is a Dmitry Komnov born May 17, 1977, in Kashira, Moscow and a Dmitry Kratov born July 16th, 1964 on the list, but Dmitry Markov, born Sept 2, 1967 is not put on the list? Who are the other Dmitry's?

Also, the other prison riot guard, Oleg Gennadievich Kuznetsov, born July 11th, 1982 is not put on the list, but a tax fraud investigator by the name of Artem Kuznetsov, born Feb 28, 1975 in Baku, Azerbaijan is placed on the list? Isn't it convenient the tax fraud investigator that was investigating Browder's tax crimes is placed on the list, but not the riot guard with the same last name that allegedly murdered Magnitsky with a rubber baton? How convenient that none of the allegations towards the dozen Russians sanctioned can be upheld in a court of law, but they are silenced from telling their stories in the West. There is no opportunity for anyone on the list to defend themselves or give their side of the story in the accusations.

So, why were the doctors put on the Magnitsky List but not the eight riot guards that allegedly beat Magnitsky to death with eight rubber batons for one hour and eighteen minutes?

Where did Browder come up with this time? Answer. It was the title of Elena Gremina's play *"One Hour Eighteen Minutes"* and one hour and eighteen minutes is the amount of time Magnitsky was left alone in the isolation cell. A Russian playwright, Elena Gremina, wrote about the medical negligence in the play *"One Hour Eighteen Minutes"* but there is no mention of eight riot guards or any beating. In fact, Browder mentions nothing about a beating the first few years talking about Sergei's death. Andrei Nekrasov, in his documentary, interviews Sergei's mother, who states he died of neglect. Andi Gross of the European Parliament stated, "you didn't take care enough", a German phrase meaning "neglect", describing his death. You can listen to interviews of Browder at several venues the first few years after Sergei's death and you hear nothing about a beating, just medical negligence. Some of those venues were the San Diego Law School, The Chatham House, and an interview on a Netherlands Podcast by Jonathan Groubert. Links to the Podcast have been removed and attempts by me to ask Mr. Groubert why this podcast has been deleted have been unsuccessful.

Dr Gaus is one of the main characters highlighted in this nine-person play, which is about her trial on the medical negligence of Magnitsky during his few hours he spent at Matrosskaya prison. From the time Magnitsky arrived at Matrosskaya at approximately 6:15 pm until his time of death that night at 9:50 pm, she would oversee his care. The translator of the play was kind enough to share with me some of the dialogue of the play, and as I mentioned before, there is nothing about a beating in this play.

The playwright writes her reason for including the real names of those accused of medical negligence is as follows: "We will present on stage all who were guilty of the hero's death: the investigators, the judges, prison guards, doctors, and give each one a monologue. We will call them by their real names and surnames. So that they can come to the theatre and look at themselves. They pass judgement and now we're judging them."

It's hard to judge the decisions of an incident that these playwrights weren't eyewitnesses to, but they appear quite emphatic in their character assassination of the surgeon, Dr Alexandra Gaus, and her fellow co-workers at the prison. Luke Harding, a journalist in London, who spent years in Russia covering stories, interviewed the playwrights, and it was an interesting interview about their experiences with the Sputnik theatre. The interview is posted on YouTube.

What I find troubling is the mismatch of the submission of alleged candidates for the Sergei Magnitsky Rule of Accountability Act and the ones who made it to Senator Ben Cardin's list.

The categories for submission to be placed on the list were defined in four different categories.

(A) responsible for detention, abuse of death of Sergei Magnitsky.
(B) Participated in efforts to conceal the legal liability for the detention, abuse of death of Sergei Magnitsky.
(C) Benefitted financially from the detention, abuse, or death of Sergei Magnitsky.
(D) Was involved in the criminal conspiracy uncovered by Sergei Magnitsky.

Clearly there's been a lot of ink put to paper examining what happened on the night Magnitsky died. What is curious to me is why Browder did not mention anything about a beating the first two years he talked about the death of his lawyer, and only mentions neglect and "we really don't know what happened to him". I mean, if I got a voicemail at midnight, a few days before Magnitsky's death of him screaming, with what sounded like he was getting beaten, I would be yelling from the rooftops. Why does he ONLY mention this voicemail in his book and has not mentioned before or after from any research I can find? I mean, wouldn't that be a slam dunk? You could trace the call or the phone, or do voice analysis or any data forensics on the call, so why never mention it? This is just another example of the strange behavior of Browder on something you would think would be the smoking gun in a case. That he only mentions with one sentence in his book is just bizarre.

No journalist is going ask about this voicemail that Browder hears on his Blackberry at 12:15 Saturday morning November 14th, 2009? If it was a call from Butyrka prison and not Matrosskaya prison (which it had to be since he wasn't moved to Matrosskaya until Monday, November 16th, 2009), why hasn't there been any attention to this obvious human rights violation from Butyrka prison? The way Browder frames the timeline around the voicemail is confusing and I believe he does this on purpose so the reader who is just casually reading doesn't catch these details. Browder says Magnitsky was transferred from Butyrka to Matrosskaya in "critical condition", but does a patient in critical condition carry his 3 bags plus 2 plastic bags under his own volition into the transport vehicle?

When Lucy Komisar asked Jamie Firestone about the voicemail at a debate, they were having at an offshore alert conference in Miami, Jamie says the voicemail was given to Scotland Yard. Still, never mentioned ever by Browder but one sentence in his book? If Browder is making the murder up, isn't this punishment to the Magnitsky family? Wouldn't they want to know their dad, husband, and son was not murdered, but had a medical incident instead? This is what bothers me most about this subject, and makes me keep an open mind there might be some truth to Browder, because who could possibly be that cruel to loved ones of the deceased? I think this paradox is the main driver sometimes of me continuing to follow this still unraveling story.

In the recent European Court of Human Rights (ECHR) judgement on the case of Magnitsky and others v Russia 11/27/2019, Dr Alexandra Gaus statement is quoted "she personally administered injections of adrenaline and atropine to the root of his tongue because it was impossible to locate any peripheral veins. They had no effect and at 9:50, the patient had been pronounced clinically dead." They sure put a lot of effort into trying to save a man's life if they were trying to murder him. In the recent *ECHR report (European Court of Human Rights)*, line items 244 and 245 give a good explanation of the events surrounding the death.

244. The Government argued the first applicant had received adequate medical assistance in the 13 November 2009 he had been taken to the prison medical unit. As soon as his medical condition had become critical on 16 November 2009, the prison officers prepared for his transfer to a prison hospital. In the late evening of the same day his condition had suddenly deteriorated and several hours later he had died.

245. The Government further stated that the investigation into the quality of medical care had been effective and thorough. In particular more than fifty witnesses had been question, and more than twenty expert examinations had been performed. They had revealed several shortcomings on the part of the medical authority. For example, there had been a significant gap in the first by the medical staff (the doctor's had not made regular entries of the first applicant's state of health); he had not received an ultrasound examination and had not been seen by a surgeon; Dr L. Had delayed the proper diagnosis; and Dr A.G had not given adequate sedation, intravenous fluid and cardio-stimulation therapy on 16 November 2009.

However, Mr Magnitsky's illness had been difficult to diagnose and there was no causal link between aforementioned shortcomings and his death. The criminal proceedings against Dr D.K on a charge of criminal negligence had ended with his acquittal. Dr L. accused of having caused the death of the first applicant, had not been held criminally liable on account of the expiry of the statutory limitation period. (End of excerpt from ECHR)

These lines in the *ECHR* show three doctors had tried to save Magnitsky's life and certainly weren't cheering for his death, yet these three doctors were placed on The Magnitsky Act sanctions list to be banned from traveling to the United States and banned from banking in the United States or accessing their assets if they owned any in the United States. Yet, the prison guards who supposedly beat Sergei for an hour and eighteen minutes, are not put on the Magnitsky list? Browder says he got a voicemail of Magnitsky being beat at Butyrka prison. Why isn't this being investigated? Wouldn't the prison guards at Butyrka on Saturday at 12:15 a.m. have more to do with human rights abuse than a surgeon and two other doctors at Matrosskaya prison?

One of the witnesses to Magnitsky's incarceration was a journalist by the name of Oleg Lurie. Lucy Komisar met this reporter in 2000 in Moscow, when they were both covering the story of the four billion missing from the IMF loan money that originated at the Republic Bank of New York. At that time Browder was still singing Putin's praises, while Oleg was a critic of the Putin government. Oleg Lurie was arrested a few years later charged with blackmailing a Duma official and was sentenced to prison in the same prison as Magnitsky. Later he was exonerated of these charges and the prosecutor apologized for the flimsy case he brought against him. While in prison he had an opportunity to talk to Magnitsky twice. The first time Magnitsky was very positive his employees were working on his case to get him out of pre-trial detention. The second time he got a chance to talk to Magnitsky was a different story. Magnitsky was very depressed and was concerned about the behavior of his legal team. They were putting pressure on him to sign a statement that placed blame on the $230 million Russian treasury theft on two cops, Karpov and Kuznetsov, who he mentions in his June 2008 police testimony. These allegations have nothing to do with the charges that Magnitsky was facing, these were two separate cases. Magnitsky's charges were about the tax fraud in Kalmykia with Saturn Investment, Dalnaya Steppe and the disabled employees, and not with the theft of Rilend, Parfenion, and Makhaon. Oleg Lurie states he was approached by someone who offered him $160,000 to bury the story about his talks with Magnitsky, but he declined. In the Prevezon video deposition, Browder is asked about this bribe, but he states he knows nothing about it and denies involvement. Oleg's testimony is a unique opportunity to see how Magnitsky's attitude changed during his eleven-month long detention, but Magnitsky did end up writing a handwritten testimony one month before his death accusing Karpov and Kuznetsov in the theft of the Russian treasury money. Was he pressured by Browder and company to write up these accusations? We will never know. I'm not sure of the credibility of Oleg, especially given that he did serve prison time, but he has made some pretty damning statements about the credibility of the Magnitsky story.

Chapter 9

MAGNITSKY IS DEAD.
THE MAGNITSKY PROJECT IS BORN

A MAN NAMED Sergei Magnitsky dies in a Russian prison and is about to become famous.

His name is added to human rights laws known as The Magnitsky Act in The United States, Canada, UK, Estonia, Lithuania and Latvia. Now in 2020, the big lobbying campaign is to pass a European Union Magnitsky Act. On December 10, 2018 on the 70th anniversary of the Universal Declaration of Human Rights (UDHR), European ministers of Foreign Affairs unanimously approved the Dutch proposal for the E.U-wide Magnitsky Act (the EU Global Human Rights Sanctions Regime). The proposal will now be developed into legislation.

Bill Browder and Vladimir Kara-Murza are the main lobbyists who have had countless meetings, both public and closed door with members of the European Parliament to gain their support. There is a common tactic Browder does to put pressure on a politician. He will bully until everyone else agrees with him, and if you don't agree with him, he will smear you as a Russian asset and can destroy your career with bad publicity. It works. Politicians cave very easily when faced with any hint of controversy to their image.

The European Parliament passed a resolution with a 447 -70 vote, calling for an EU-wide "Magnitsky-Act" to include state and non-state actors who have contributed, physically, financially or through acts of systemic corruption, to such abuse and crimes, worldwide. During the debate about the name of the resolution, the Vice-President of the European Parliament, Heidi Hautula, was against having one individual's name tied to the Act. Her disapproval was not towards the Act itself, just the semantics of the name of the Act. This brought a relentless assault of smears against her by Browder on social media. I myself became a very small part of this story when I tweeted out support of Heidi's position. On Twitter it became a three day back and forth which brought in other "Browder truthers" who I interact with frequently on Twitter. All of us were called Russian trolls by two anonymous Twitter accounts that analyze data. My friend on Twitter, Tony, calls this argument "analysis paralysis" which I think is the perfect term. Bill Browder would retweet data analysis accounts stating, "See? These are the troll farms in St Petersburg who come for me on Twitter. I must be really getting under the skin of Putin!" I'm paraphrasing, but you get the gist. This rebuttal delights his followers and they will call Heidi all sorts of names and soon, a vote that had many more against attaching a specific victim's name to a human rights act, slowly changes to more politicians in the 'yes' column for a specific name, and less in the 'No' column against a specific name attached to the human rights law.

It is very effective. He launched lies about Heidi calling her Andrei Nekrasov' "girlfriend", which Andrei denied. He has no shame in the ad hominem attacks against parliamentary members. Andrei Nekrasov' wife died of cancer a few years ago and I surmise the personal attacks are not easy for him to deal with it. I'm sure he is still grieving his collaborator and spouse's death. Browder is shameless with his pressure. When Stef Blok from the Minister of Foreign Affairs in the Netherlands raised some questions, Browder sent out what I believe is a threat to him if he didn't back Browder. Browder tweets, "Being against the Magnitsky Act is often a career ruining position. @minsterBlok should study what happened to former Canadian Foreign Minister Stephanie Dion for vociferously blocking Magnitsky in Canada. This is an issue where morality sweeps away realpolitik w/o apology". Browder effectively ruined Ms. Dion's career because she didn't "toe the line".

Even Nataliya Veselnitskaya was thrown into the debate when someone tagged her into the conversation. This was the same position she had in her critique of The Magnitsky Act, not in opposition to the Act itself, just in opposition to the name of someone she thought was corrupt being on a piece of legislature. In December 2012, The Magnitsky Act, which repeals the Jackson-Vanik amendment, was signed into law by President Obama. Jackson-Vanik amendment is named after the original co-sponsors, two Democratic Senators. Say if someone at the time argued against the name of Jackson or Vanik on the amendment, not the body of the amendment, but just having two names attached to it, I'm sure they may have been met with smears as well.

Browder states in his recent University of Chicago speech that the Obama administration were reluctant to have Browder pursue amending the Jackson-Vanik at the legislature level. He said he was more effective in the halls of Congress, than he was with Obama administration. I'm not sure what Browder's feelings were about Hillary Clinton, but I know he called John Kerry "Putin's lapdog" for his appeasement policies towards Russia in annexation of Crimea, Syria, and other policy positions. Browder is vocal about the initial resistance he received in the Obama administration during his campaign for the Act. Michael McFaul was in the Obama administration and his telling of the events around this Magnitsky Act is especially interesting. If you read pages 364-371of his book "From Cold War to Hot Peace", you get his version of events which I notice has a sleight of hand approach, the same tactics I see in books like *Red Notice*. He says he debated the merits of repealing The Jackson-Vanik Amendment back in high school in 1979, but then goes on to say, "He thinks it worked". He states, "historians have debated whether Jackson-Vanik worked on not". So, this is a contradiction in just a few sentences. Why is he saying he was advocating repealing a policy that was effective? This word play, and his carefully constructed explanation of his positions and conversations over the years 2011-2012 with Bill Browder is well crafted revisionism if I have ever read any. The Obama administration were supportive of Russia joining the World Trade Organization, but if we were still applying trade restrictions, America would be in noncompliance with our WTO obligations. These were issues the Obama administration needed to address with their support of Russia joining the WTO. There was no political will in Congress to have a Senate vote, on what looked like, appeasement to Russia. Repealing the Act without "getting anything in return" looked weak. McFaul then says, "And then our legislator experts discovered a lifeline-The Magnitsky Act." Read that again. "And then our legislator experts discovered a lifeline-The Magnitsky Act." Page 364 of "From Cold War to Hot Peace". McFaul says at first he wanted to make policy at the Executive level, or, as he says "Moved by Browder's passion, I began working on a U.S government response. I quickly learned that we could put people on our visa-ban list for human rights violations, without enacting new legislation. In fact, President Obama strengthened our authority to do so, with an executive order he signed in August 2011. We had the intelligence community, State Department, and Treasury scrutinize the list that Browder had given me to see if we had enough evidence to make these individuals subject to our visa ban. Of the sixty or so people on Bill's list, we identified an initial dozen to ban from travel to the United States. After considerable deliberation, we simply did it, but without making our action public." He then goes on to say this wasn't enough for Browder, he was persistent. Then McFaul says the list leaked so now was public, and that still wasn't enough for Browder. So, "when Obama meets Putin in Los Cabos, Mexico, he explains he's going to sign the Jackson-Vanik/PNTR bill and Putin says he'll come up with an equivalent list" which McFaul said, "sounded fine to him". Now, this whole explanation is fascinating, because as we know, Putin's government's response to the passing of the bill was to put Michael McFaul on their own sanctions list. Also, if you read the names on the initial list, I mean, what? Really? These are the people the State Department agonized over and scrutinized? Out of the twelve, four were doctors at the prison trying to save a man's life? I just shake my head at the absurdity of the whole situation. All to protect a fable invented by Browder. We know Browder put political pressure on anyone that did not follow his marching orders and a politician as powerful as Hillary Clinton was no exception. A leaked Podesta email of Hillary's campaign itinerary shows she was able to squash a negative story that Bloomberg News was going to put out that she was too 'Russia friendly', with her husband giving half a million-dollar speeches in Moscow. Part of the email reads "We killed a story trying to link HRC's opposition to Magnitsky bill to a $500,000 speech that WJC gave in Moscow" WJC, is of course, William Jefferson Clinton, and I'm going to guess Browder is the one threatening a politician to get them behind him or else he will smear them through his usual friendly papers. This has been his modus operandi for decades. As you know the company Clinton spoke to was Renaissance Capital, the company that was allegedly behind the 2006 Russian treasury theft with one of its subsidiaries. So, Browder wasted no time heading over to the Henry Jackson Society in London to work on getting help writing up the proposals for the repeal of the Jackson-Vanik Amendment. After Hillary lost the Presidential election to Donald Trump, the blame game got crazy. Her enthusiastic supporter, Lyn De Rothschild, on Twitter, blamed Podesta. Podesta blamed Russia, and Hillary and Bill became the biggest Russo phobic personalities in America.

Browder is a master at media manipulation and dominated the

narrative. After Magnitsky died he began a media campaign to highlight the injustice of his death. He appears on Fox News and CNN and gives his story to newspaper outlets like Bloomberg, Financial Times and The Moscow Times.

12/15/09 "I don't know whether they killed him deliberately or if he died of neglect"

12/6/2010 "They put him in a straitjacket, put him in an isolation room, and waited outside the door until he died"

12/13/11 "They put him in an isolation cell, tied him to a bed, and then allowed eight riot guards to beat him with rubber batons until he was dead"

You notice the first two years no mention of violence. Later, Browder was appearing to have two versions of the story depending on what country the reporter was from. With Russian and European journalists, he didn't mention the beating, and with U.S media, he would emphasize the beating. At no point does he mention the voicemail he received on his Blackberry two days before Magnitsky died. In 2010, Browder told Nekrasov "he didn't know how Magnitsky died", and never once mentions the voicemail to him. Nekrasov stating "It's an absurd lie for more than one reason."

The first four months there is no mention of Sergei being the whistleblower either. This storyline does not appear until March 2009, at the same time the Rimma Starova whistleblowing disappears from the Hermitage website. In the documentary, *The Magnitsky Act*, Andrei Nekrasov asks Bill Browder about seventy-year old Rimma Starova, and Browder responds saying "she's just a pensioner". Seems like a funny way to talk about the women who was in charge of liquidating your multimillion-dollar companies and is the CEO of your offshore company in the British Virgin Islands, but this is his immediate response to any inquiry about Rimma Starova.

In 2015, Browder's non-fiction book *Red Notice* is launched, and Browder has a script he will have to follow from here on out. In some ways it complicates things for Browder, as he has to stick with the "eight riot guards beat Magnitsky for one hour and eighteen minutes" line and can no longer spin a different story to Russian and European reporters. Browder has been getting more push back to his narrative in Europe than the United States, precisely because they are more likely to see the contradictions in his previous European interviews. A Danish newspaper, *Finans*, published an article critical of Browder. Browder formally complained to the Danish Press Council, and council ruled in favor of the two journalists, Jette Aagaard and Kristoffer Brahm, finding "no errors in their critical coverage of Bill Browder".

The only big-name journalist in America who came close to writing about some of the contradictions in the Magnitsky Story was NBC News Correspondent covering national security, Ken Dillanian. Lucy Komisar has talked extensively about Ken Dillanian's discovery of the added paragraph in the WSJ article that said Magnitsky was a whistleblower. Ken was asking Browder some questions in an email correspondence about the English translation of the Russian human rights reports and Browder responded it was a "clerical error". Yes, Browder claims an entire paragraph that never existed before but magically appears in the English translation of the human rights report is a "clerical error".

Ken Dillanian was going to do an exposè on The Magnitsky story with a proposed release date May 2016, and after the back and forth with Browder in emails, Browder's lawyers sent a letter to NBC threatening a lawsuit if they ran with the story, so it was shelved. Ken Dillanian never ran the May 2016 exposé, but he did retweet Lucy Komisar's article written September 2017, that detailed the added paragraph in the *Wall Street Journal* English translation of the human rights report. Lucy discovered the added paragraph when she read the human rights report submitted to the U.S government in the *Prevezon*

Magnitsky is dead. The Magnitsky Project is Born

vs US case. She discovered through PACER (Public access to court electronics records) that the court document submitted did not have the paragraph of Magnitsky blowing the whistle that the Wall Street Journal version had. She realized the same thing as Dillanian who read the Russian language version of the human rights report. (or his NBC Russian translators did). I decided to get access to PACER to read the court documents in the case myself, and now have the ability to read all the submitted documents in the *Prevezon vs US* case.

Lucy was aware of the conversations between Ken Dillanian and William Browder, not because Ken offered up this information, but because the emails were in the public sphere when a batch of a State Department employee's emails got hacked. Russian expert, Robert Otto, had his emails leaked to the web and his back and forth with Ken Dillanian could be read. Robert Otto was also Cc'd into a lot of William Browder's emails to various Washington D.C players. It became apparent with reading the leaked emails of Robert Otto that he was skeptical of Browder's version of events. When he was talking to his boss at the State Department, John Williams, they joked about Browder and his authenticity. Robert Otto quoted the famous line from the film "*The Man who Shot Liberty Valance,*" "When the Legend becomes fact, print the legend," meaning, Robert Otto at the State Department was willing to go along with Bill Browder's story.

This wasn't even the most concerning email of Robert Otto's about Browder and The Magnitsky Story. Bill Browder Bcc'd Robert Otto into an email he sent to Kyle Parker, a US congressional staffer and key drafter of the Magnitsky Act. Kyle has been the chief of staff of the *U.S. Helsinki Commisssion* since December 2017. In July 2018, he was one of the ten U.S diplomats Russia requested to question. In the email Browder sends to Kyle Parker, with Robert Otto Bcc'd into, is a picture of Nataliya Veselnitskaya's house in Russia. The date of the email is Monday, June 6th, 2016 and the subject line is "subject: FW Veselnitksaya house". Below the picture of her house is the name

Ivan Cherkasov, Hermitage Capital Management, and the address of Hermitage Capital Management in London.

What is significant about this date is that this was right before she traveled to the United States for the infamous Trump Tower meeting. She also traveled to New York for meetings with Glenn Simpson in regard tothe Prevezon case in New York. When Lee Stranahan, a radio host for a *Sputnik* a.m. radio program, interviewed Ms Veselnitskaya, she said she had no idea her house was being photographed.

Browder was effective at having Ms. Veselnitskaya portrayed as the villain in the U.S eyes. When he appears on Fox News, he emphasized her meetings with Fusion GPS founder Glenn Simpson, and how she met him both before and after the meeting at Trump Tower. He implies to Fox viewers this meeting is a set up by the DNC to try to "dirty up" the Trump campaign with yet another Russia connection. When Browder appears on CNN he talks about how Paul Manafort is working for Victor Yanukovych, former President of Ukraine who is a "Putin puppet" and talks about Ms Veselnitskaya's close relationship with the Putin regime. This is an extremely effective media campaign as it's easy to say 'Putin and Trump are bad' to CNN and 'Putin and DNC are bad' to Fox. There are only softball questions asked of Browder on all media outlets, whether they are bias towards the Democratic or the Republican Party. Like in the halls of Congress, Browder can hold court quite easily. He actually will become quite giddy when he describes the power a human rights story can have to get Congress to all agree on something. In a recent panel talk at University of Chicago, he lets his guard down, talking about the enormous influence he yields.

Ms Veselnitskaya never had a chance to tell her side of the story effectively. In what was a masterful hit piece by NBC in their interview of her, they would translate her words with far more nefarious intent than the original Russian version of the answer to the question. Nataliya's emails were hacked prior to her interview and they were given to *Open Russia*, a dropbox kind of like Wikileaks that the NGO Open Russia provides for hackers to share their data. (Open Russia is now renamed openDemocracy) When she was shown her emails during the interview and asked why she was corresponding with the Putin government, she insisted, as a private attorney, it was not unusual to ask for Federal government assistance in obtaining documents or other clerical hoops one went through when preparing a case. When asked why she was going to speak to Trump Jr, she described herself as a kind of whistleblower about Browder, but the English translation was saying she was an "informant".

Now, I ask you, do you think she would answer the question saying she was essentially "a spy" for the Russian government? Do you really think she would answer the question in this way? I don't. I found her lengthier interview with Lee Stranahan where he gave her a chance to really tell her side of the story, much more interesting. During the NBC hit piece on Nataliya, they also interviewed Mikhail Khodorkovsky, the founder of Open Russia media sharing. He is critical of the Russian lawyer who is doing nothing more than representing her client in a civil case in NYC and supporting a film that challenged Browder's narrative. We know there were attempts by Russia to find out information about the Ziff brothers; Dirk, Edward and Daniel. US Treasury officials were sending emails back and forth to HotMail and Gmail accounts set up by Russians to exchange information during the Obama administration. At least ten FinCEN employees (Financial Crimes Enforcement Network) filed formal whistleblower complaints about these exchanges. They warned, "communicating on Gmail made the treasury's internal systems vulnerable to fishing expeditions", but staff continued using back channels into 2017. A Treasury spokesperson states they reported the incidents in July and August 2016 to the Inspector General's office. One senior adviser quit in anger and has been arrested and accused of releasing financial records to a journalist. Natalie Mayflower Edwards told congressional staffers FinCEN withheld documents revealing suspicious transaction of Trump associates that the committee had requested. Who was she referring to? Jared Kushner's relationship with the Ziff brothers? Who knows. Did she think connecting those two would harm Trump, as she was known to be against his Presidency. If you think along partisan lines you will never understand this story. If you think New York billionaires know other New York billionaires and they fight like preschoolers sometimes, you will understand this story. On 12/20/19, BuzzFeed wrote about the Obama administration's back channel communications to Russia's inquiry about the Ziff brothers. Browder tweets out the same day, "Russian agents used the pretext of fighting ISIS to dupe U.S Treasury officials to pass on information about me and the Ziff brothers in 2016 as part of their campaign to destroy me and roll back the Magnitsky Act." Remember, Russia and the United States have a Mutual Legal Assistance Treaty signed by Bill Clinton, so cooperating on investigations is not unusual. If Browder and Ziff are innocent, why so much effort to sabotage sharing data? Wouldn't this help strengthen his case to cooperate? During Nataliya Veselnitskaya's testimony she was asked if she was aware that Glenn Simpson was also working on opposition research about the Trump campaign. She replied the first time she ever heard about his research was in a letter by Chuck Grassley on March 31st 2017 that was published by the Daily Beast on the same day his office released the statement. BuzzFeed and The Daily Beast have been sycophant news outlets for the Magnitsky hoax. Do you remember when Diane Feinstein released Glenn Simpson's testimony? She stated she "had a cold" and the media didn't care because they thought, if it hurts Trump, who cares. Is it possible she wanted to expose Browder and it had nothing to do with Trump? Her good friend, Ron Dellums, was a lobbyist for this Trump Tower motley crew of Rinat and Nataliya. When Ron Dellums passed away Diane Feinstein tweeted out "A Marine, social worker, councilman, 13-term congressman and mayor, Ron Dellums lived to serve others. I will never forget his courage, or the pride which he represented California and the East Bay. My deepest condolences to his loved ones. We will miss him". Was it possible politicians get stuck in the middle of these Browder lies, not knowing how to turn, so when Grassley and Feinstein looked shell shocked in front of the cameras after that closed door session, it was opposite what a partisan mind may think? Remember, Anatoli Samachovnov, who attended the Trump Tower meeting as Ms Veselnitskaya's interpreter, had also helped translate for Hillary Clinton, John Kerry, and Barack Obama in their official capacities meeting with Russian officials in the past. Anatoli had been contracted to the State Department for over twenty years and helped translate Sergei Lavrov exchanges frequently. Do we really think these were "spies"? Why was Ms Veselnitskaya such a threat? When you read her written testimony submitted to the Senate Judiciary Committee answering their questions, it becomes quite clear why Browder would want her side of the story blacklisted.

Chapter 10

ARE VESELNITSKAYA AND RIMMA THE REAL WHISTLEBLOWERS?

WHAT WAS IN Ms Veselnitskaya's testimony and Glenn Simpson's testimony to the Senate Judiciary Committee that Browder wanted kept quiet? It turns out, that not only was Ms Veselnitskaya exposing the 2013 conviction of Browder in the tax evasion case, she was also claiming he and Sergei Magnitsky were behind the 2007 $230 million Russian treasury theft. This is a bold claim, but she does not come to this conclusion lightly, but presents a lot of logical facts that could give even an ardent supporter of Browder some pause to want to investigate further. This is the part of the story that is most difficult to follow, because money laundering, is by its nature, a very complex web of money layering. Anonymous companies are used as tax havens located in countries like Cyprus, British Virgin Islands, and Panama, and anonymous bank accounts hold the money. The amount of companies, banks, and people accused by Browder to be involved in the Russian treasury theft would make your head spin. If you combined all the accusations and connections, it looks like a Jackson Pollock painting.

Veselnitskaya does an excellent job breaking through some of the disinformation Browder has spread, but for some, they will never look at objectively because they think she is either being used by the Russian government feeding her disinformation, or she is willfully engaging in spreading lies to help her client. I think she is doing neither and open sources will confirm her statements. In fact, the person who gives the most credibility to her statements is none other than Sergei Magnitsky himself in his 2008 police testimony.

I'm going to get in the weeds a bit here, but I hope when you see the main point I'm going to try to convey is that Hermitage Capital Management was always in control of their "stolen companies", and therefore, were most likely behind the Russian treasury theft. It's hard to be 100% sure of anything. As Voltaire states, "Doubt is not a pleasant condition, but certainty is absurd", so I'm not certain, but I will show why I think this is true.

Let's start with Rimma Starova, the whistleblower on the companies in question being stolen. Browder calls her a pensioner, but he never denies he knew she was the CEO of the company that was in charge of liquidating OOO Rilend, OOO Parfenion, and OOO Makhaon.

In her statement July 2008 she says to police, **"In relation to these Pavlov A.A., Turukhina A.S, Yakovlev K.A, Shulgina E.N., Maivrova Y.M., Matlseve E.A and E.M. Khairetdinov can explain that these person were lawyers, representing in arbitration courts OOO (Makhaon), OOO (Parfenion), OOO (Rilend), OOO (Instar), OOO (Gran-Active)- ZAO (Logos Plus) Foreign companies Kone Holdings Limited and Glendora Holdings Limited, asked him for compensation OOO (Pluton) and find new General Directors of the companies OOO (Parfenion), OOO (Makhaon) OOO (Rilend) In order to give legal force made documents, an unidentified person asked Markelov V.A, not knowledgeable about criminal intent, to arrange for the obtaining of decisions of the arbitration court confirming**

the debt of 000 (Makhaon), 000 (Parfenion), and 000 (Rilend)."
(End of excerpt from Rimma Starova testimony)

So what do these three paragraph excerpts from Ms Starova's testimony to the police mean? Well, if she is a credible witness, they are pretty damaging to Browder and his employees. One of Hermitage's employees is a man named Eduard M. Khairetdinov, and Rimma Starova is saying he was one of the lawyers representing the supposedly stolen companies, R/P/M (Rilend, Parfenion, and Makhaon), in arbitration courts. She also names A.A. Pavlov as one of the lawyers. Lucy Komisar has interviewed the lawyer, Andrei Pavlov, and he admits he helped run the treasury theft for both Hermitage Capital Management and Renaissance Capital but he will not say who his client was. Pavlov also told Lucy that Markelov told him something important, that Sergei Magnitsky brought papers to Markelov. That's a lot of hearsay, so I'm not saying anything is accurate in the statements, just documenting that Pavlov has stated Sergei brought documents to Markelov.

As far as the second paragraph in Rimma's testimony, she says Kone Holding Limited and Glendora Holdings Limited asked him to find new General Directors for the companies R/P/M. If this is true, this again implicates Browder and company. Once again, the ever-brilliant Lucy Komisar, puts the pieces together and explains that Kone and Glendora were Cyprus shell companies that owned Browder's Russian shells, who in turn were owned by another offshore entity. It's called 'layering', the classic money laundering technique. Kone and Glendora were in Cyprus for the benefit of the dual taxation treaty that allowed a cut in Russian taxes for companies by Cyprus enterprises that invested in Russia. Browder doesn't have an enterprise in Cyprus, just shell companies, therefore these shell 'pass-through' companies are a scam. These scams are worth millions of evaded tax dollars.

In the third paragraph excerpt of Rimma Starova's July 2008 statement, she states an unidentified person asks Markelov to arrange for obtaining the decision of the arbitration court, confirming the debt of R/P/M. Who was the unidentified person?

With Starova's testimony, we begin to wonder if Eduard Khairetdinov and Kone and Glendora were in on the Russian treasury theft. She is not the only person giving sworn statements. Another person giving sworn statements would give her testimony more weight, and this is when we look at Sergei Magnitsky's testimony to police, which is probably the most damaging of all to Browder's narrative. Browder has made Magnitsky practically Mother Theresa, so we should think his sworn testimony should be important to read. Let's take a look at what he has to say…

Chapter 11

Is Magnitsky a whistleblower?

We know Browder's version from *Red Notice* and his endless appearances in media. Sergei was a whistleblower of the crooked cops, Karpov and Kuznetsov, that stole the companies working with the Klyuev gang to steal $230 million from the Russian treasury. This story has been a New York Times best seller and has been translated into dozens of languages. It has long descriptions of seedy, smoky hotel rooms, and woman that are eager to bed Mr Browder. It "reads like a novel but it's all true!" This is stated over and over in book reviews by famous people, including Lee Child's review on the front cover.

A neatly packaged video campaign titled "Untouchables" claims Karpov and Kuznetsov lived in luxury after the theft buying yachts, mansions, and luxury cars. With the saturation of one man's version of events, it's an unpopular position to look further into the story, but I think it's important to get clarification of Magnitsky's testimony. It turns out Browder lied a lot about Karpov. He wasn't making six thousand a year, he was making six thousand a month. Also, he didn't buy his house after the theft, he purchased the land in 2004 and was in the process of building during that time. He actually had to sell his flat in Moscow for legal expenses in trying to sue Browder for libel in London. Browder was nervous about the libel case and did everything he could to get the case dismissed. One of the most unusual events surrounding the libel case was Nataliya Veselnitskaya was approached by Pussy Riot's lawyer, Mark Feygin. He said to her if she found dirt on Karpov, they'd be willing to drop the case against her client, Denis Katsyv, in the New York courts. She declined his offer and submitted an affidavit into the New York Courts about this offer by Mark Feygin. Anyone can read her statement on PACER. These were cases in London and New York involving Hermitage mind you. Let's now travel back to Moscow for Mr. Magnitsky's questioning in the Russian Treasury theft.

Case #374015 is what brought Sergei Magnitsky to sit in front of S.E Gordiyevsky, an attorney and investigator for the Public Prosecution Office of the Russian Federation for the City of Moscow. Case #374015 concerned the circumstances of issuance of the Powers of Attorney to Mr. E.M Khairetdinov, the authority issued to him on behalf of 000 "Parfenion, 000"Makhaon" and 000"Rilend" as of October 17, 2007. Remember, 000 R/P/M is the renaming of the new companies on the second pyramid. Draw two pictures of each pyramid to keep track, it helps.

E.M Khairetdinov is a lawyer who works for Hermitage Capital Management, Browder's company in Russia. He is tall with a mustache, and the man Andrei Nekrasov approached at the *Red Notice* book launch in New York. He is the one when asked about the complaints made to The Russian Federation about the theft of the companies called it an "alibi", which is an odd choice of words. This exchange is on video and can be seen in the documentary "The Magnitsky Act". During Magnitsky's police questioning he is asked about Khairetdinov being given the powers of attorney for, what at this point, is supposed to be control over the stolen Hermitage companies R/P/M. Magnitsky reports he found out about the stolen companies on Tuesday 16th, 2007, and there was going to be an arbitration hearing with fake employees on Monday, October 22nd, 2007. Magnitsky explains it was imperative to get a "real" representative to the hearing to expose the scam.

Magnitsky states the following: **"On Tuesday 16 October 2007, it became known the lawsuits filed with the Arbitration Court of Saint Petersburg and Leningrad region against Parfenion LLC and Makhaon LLC and the nearest court hearing to cover one of the cases was scheduled the morning of 22 October 2007. Therefore a representative was needed to attend a hearing as a matter of urgency. Since the lawyer E.M had already represented interests of I.S. Cherkasov, director general of Kameya LLC, the latter made an arrangement with him for the representation of interests on behalf of three companies, namely Parfenion LLC, Reland LLC, and Makhaon LLC. On 17 October 2007, Cherkasov informed me that the director generals of those three companies, Paul Wrench and Martin Wilson, signed powers of attorney and sent them to Firestone Duncan (CIS) limited branch in Moscow by a DHL courier. I have retained a copy of receipt 395 1055 102 for DHL parcel which carried the powers of attorney to the destination. The receipt says that the documents were out on 17 October 2007 from the Isle of Guernsey, the sender indicated as M. Wilson, HSBC Management (GCY). If necessary a copy of the receipt may be provided. I believe that the draft texts of the power of attorney in favor of the lawyer E.M. Khairetdinov were prepared by V.G Kleiner, I.S Cherkasov and other Russian speaking staff at the office, dispatched to Paul Wrench and Martin Wilson, signed by them and sent back to Firestone Duncan in Moscow. After the powers of attorney were received they were sealed with the replica seals produced (after the original seals had been impounded) and kept at Firestone Duncan and conveyed to the lawyer E.M. Khairetdinov."** "I knew about the arbitration hearing on 16 October 2007. He states he had in depth knowledge of the activities pursued by all three companies but I had no idea of their relationship to Logos Plus, Closed Joint Stock Company, which is why I was surprised to know of such massive lawsuits were filed and considered in conjunction with fraud, since, as it followed from the rulings dated 3 and 7 September 2007 by the Arbirtration Court of Saint Petersburg and Leningrad". "Right away I report these documents and details to I.S. Cherkasov and V.G Kleiner, he is now working and worked in the London office of Hermitage Capital at this point. They felt indignant and requested that statements be received from the United State Register of Legal Entities regarding Kamea LLC, Parfenion LLC, and Makhaon LLC. The statements came in on 18 October 2008….." (END of excerpts from Magnitsky's testimony)

So what does Magnitsky's statement mean? He confirms E.M. Khairetdinov is given powers of attorney of "stolen companies" backing up Rimma Starova testimony. Magnitsky tries to spin it that Khairetdinov is only given power of attorney to try to stop a scam in progress. This doesn't make any sense as wouldn't someone like Browder mention this publicly and not wait until they got confirmation by the United State Register of Legal Entities an entire year later?

Magnitsky also says he told the Hermitage employees, Kleiner and Cherkasov, about the arbitration court dates and says they felt "indignant" and Kleiner and Cherkasov needed to pursue findings through the Ukraine Register. The findings came back a year later confirming the theft. What? This doesn't make any sense. So, these guys knew the companies were stolen for a whole year and never went to the media? Browder? The guy who has dozens of journalists and politicians on speed dial never mentions these court hearings?

Lucy Komisar says that Browder knew out about the stolen companies even earlier than October 2007 because The Hermitage website shows HSBC set aside millions of dollars for the task of regaining the companies.

Who would I believe, Browder or Magnitsky after reading Magnitsky's testimony? Magnitsky basically admits they knew companies were stolen and Browder's employee, Khairetdinov, was given powers of attorney over the companies October 17, 2007 to represent them in court. The same thing Rimma Starova said, "Pavlov and Khairetdinov were lawyers in the arbitration courts." (paraphrased)

Magnitsky tried to wiggle out of being involved saying the police had the original seals (they took them during the raid on offices) and he, Magnitsky, only had duplicate seals at Firestone Duncan so he couldn't have been involved. The problem with this is an expert witness said in the Russian courts, duplicate seals were used in the arbitration hearings for the theft, not the originals. Also, you read he admits the duplicate seals were used to give Khairetindov the powers of attorney. Magnitsky himself says Karpov offered to return seals when employees of Firestone Duncan requested their return in November and December 2007, however, V.G Kleiner and I.S Cherkasov requested that the seals from Karpov' office not be retrieved unless criminal proceeding were instituted to investigate the illegal re registration of the companies.

During the Prevezon case, Katsyv' team gave the US government a document submitted in defense of Denis Katsyv, the owner of Prevezon. Some of the excerpts of the document are outlined as follows, beginning with a description of Sergei Magnitsky being co-executor for the scam.

"As co -executor of the fraudulent scheme and having the most complete data on financial activities of Makhaon, Rilend, and Parfenion, S.L. Magnitsky calculated the sum of the tax allegedly overpaid to the budget, prepared sales tax returns and primary accounting documents, confirming them, certified them with duplicate seals, then handed them to O.G Gasanov and V.A Markelov, who together with V.N. Kurochkin and S.M Korobeynikov used them to misinform tax authorities and steal the 5.4 billion rubles.

S.M. Korobeynikov in his turn, as the owner of CB "Universal Savings Bank", opened accounts for the organization, deposited the money stolen from the budget under the guise of a tax refund and contributed to subsequent legitimization thereof (transfer to to other banks and other credit institutions of the Russian Federation and the subsequent transfer of the money abroad.) Based on the documents prepared by S.L. Magnitsky, Federal Tax Service Inspectorate No 25 and No 28 made a decision on tax refund in the amount of 5,409,503,006.48 rubles, which on December 26th, 2007 was transferred to the accounts of the companies by the Federal treasury of the Ministry of Finance of the Russian Federation. Another change of legal owner of Rilend, Makhaon, and Parfenion (Pluto LLC) to a new front Boily Systems (British Virgin Islands) E.M Khairetdinov arranges secret withdraws from tax authorities of the forged documents prepare by S.L. Magnitsky and used by O.G Gasanov, V.A Markelov to steal the 5.4 billion rubles and subsequently keeps them at his place. Following the discovery of a number of specific tax documents during a search at E.M Khairetdinov, the latter left the territory of the Russian Federation and according to the available information is still in the U.K were since 2006-2007 the majority of people from Browder's group engaged in a multi year system organized fraudulent activity have been hiding out.

By decisions of Tverskoy District Court of the City of Moscow dated April 28, 2009 and March 10, 2011 Markelov and Khlebnikov were found guilty of committing a crime specified in Part 4 of article 159, large scale complex fraud. They were sentenced five years in prison. Money in the amount of 685,024,893,29 was forfeited to the State Investigations into the stealing of the 5.4 billion rubles in respect o Kurochkin, Korobeinikov, Gasanov, and S.L. Magnitsky was discontinued owing to the deaths. E.M. Khairetdinov was put on the wanted list." (End of statement)

This statement is saying Magnitsky worked with Gasanov and Markelov to work the tax fraud. It also states it wasn't $230 million but $218,834,569 US dollars at the exchange rate of the day of the fraud December 26, 2007, but hey, aren't we splitting hairs on this detail?

Then the Russian government continues saying that the accusations towards the cops, Karpov and Kuznetsov, are not true. It states by the time Karpov took up the case, the raid and seizures of documents/seals already occurred. Also it describes how Investigator Silchenko arrested Magnitsky, not Karpov or Kuznetsov. Silchenko was not connected to Karpov and Kuznetsov. Karpov did not prosecute Magnitsky for tax evasion. The criminal case against Magnitsky was only conducted by Kuznetsov in the initial stage. After the period of imprisonment, Kuznetsov no longer conducted operational activities and had nothing to do with the case. In fact, when Karpov sued Browder in London for libel, the case was not taken up by the courts because the Judge deemed it outside their jurisdiction. The judge however stated, "the causal link between arrest and death is lacking completely and there is no evidence of torture and murder" and that "the defendants adduced no evidence to prove their warrant in libel". Now Karpov is on the UK Magnitsky Act sanction list, so Karpov can't travel to London to protest Browder talking smack about him on UK morning cooking shows. Browder spun the case as a "victory", but it was just a case the courts declined to take. Same as when Rinat Akhmetshin sued Browder for libel in America.

The document then goes on to talk about the reason for a pre-trial detention of Magnitsky was justified since it was established, he obtained a visa to London and was a flight risk, threatened witnesses, and took steps to conceal and destroy evidence. ECHR (European Courts of Human Rights) confirms this document's statements with their own conclusion. "The Court concludes that the first applicant's (Magnitsky's) arrest was not arbitrary, and that it was based on reasonable suspicion of him having committed a criminal offense. Accordingly, this complaint (by the Magnitskys) is manifestly ill-founded within the meaning of Article 35 3 (a) of the Convention, and must be rejected pursuant to Article 35 4 (205)" - The European Court of Human Rights. The ECHR went on to say his pretrial detention was justified: The court ruled this since Magnitsky booked tickets to Kyiv and they were unable to find him at his place of residence. The court found evidence relevant about Magnitsky being involved in sham employment, paying money for it, and giving instructions on how to behave if interrogated by the authorities. The Court further observed that the District court also justified Mr Magnitsky's detention by reference to "… the gravity of the charges and the risk of influencing witnesses, absconding, or reoffending".

Another Browder claim was that Magnitsky was the first Russian citizen convicted posthumously in history. Untrue. ECHR states, **"In view of the clarification by the Constitutional Court on the right of the deceased defendants family to rehabilitation, and in response to numerous complaints, publications, statements in the press and in various media outlets a case opened in the Tversky District Court and after six months reviewed each evidence to which the preliminary investigative agency and the prosecutor referred in their report, and revealing the full involvement of S.L. Magnitsky to the offenses W.F. Browder was accused, denied S.L. Magnitsky posthumous rehabilitation having terminated the criminal case against him (ruling of the Tversky District Court of the City of Moscow July 11, 2013)"** In other words, they only reviewed his case because the family requested rehabilitation of the deceased in attempt to drop the charges posthumously. On this same date, W.F Browder was found guilty of a multimillion deliberate tax evasion and sentenced to nine years of imprisonment and put on the federal and international wanted list. The defense lawyers for Browder and Magnitsky were court appointed, as Magnitsky's family boycotted the hearings calling them corrupt. (Even though they initially sought rehabilitation).

The document submitted in Prevezon case continues to go line by line through all the accusations by Browder with links to the rulings in the Russian courts. One of the most interesting points it mentions is the arbitration court hearing after the 2007 treasury theft. Hermitage was trying to get companies back under Hermitage control. It points out at no time during any of these arbitration hearings does it say Mr. O.G Gasanov stole the companies. "There were no allegations of falsification of power of attorney or forgery made by the claimants" (Claimants being Hermitage).

So, Gasanov had the authority to have Cyprus companies Kone and Glendora give companies to Pluton, who gave companies to British Virgin Island based company Boily Systems on July 2, 2007. Oh! Guess who was in charge of Boily Systems? None other than Ms Rimma Starova, a seventy year old pensioner in a town in Russia. Can you see why she blew the whistle after reading about the charges against Browder in the paper in April 2008? Would you want to be the last one holding the hot potato when the police catch up to the scam? If you are confused. You should be. (Look at your pyramid drawings!) It's very confusing and designed that way to layer money to avoid paying taxes. Crazy, right? Would you give up your citizenship, set up offshore companies, fake LLCs with fake employees to just "stick it to the man"? Yeah, I wouldn't either, even if it saved me millions, because, the crooked world of high finance isn't something we can comprehend.

The way Browder tries to explain why his lawyer's office were being raided is probably the hardest to swallow narrative in this whole story, but let's hear it. So, Eduard Khairetdinov' office was raided August 2008, and charges were brought against him for his part in the tax heist. How can he explain his innocence with being caught red handed with all the documents? Well, you can read *Red Notice* to find out his explanation, or I can tell you now. Browder pulls out all the stops with this scenario. Are you ready?

So, let's just say I was a police officer questioning Browder.

Cop: "Browder, how do you explain how your lawyer Eduard Khairetdinov had all the evidence incriminating you, Magnitsky, and others hiding in his office?

Browder: "It was planted"

Cop: "Planted you say, how?"

Browder: "Yes planted. A DHL parcel was sent from London and arrived 90 minutes before the raid and it contained all the fake documents incriminating me."

Cop: "How do you know this?"

Browder: "Because when my team and I found out a DHL was sent from our Hermitage Capital Management address to Ed's Moscow office we went to the local DHLs and asked if there was a package with our return address sent on that date, and we discovered there was. So we looked at the CCTV footage and saw two Eastern European looking guys stuffing documents from a plastic bag into the DHL parcel."

Cop "And did you identify them?"

Browder: "Well, we looked closely and saw the plastic bag they carried with the fake documents had the logo of a popular retail store in Kazan, Tatarstan, so we knew they were the crooks. We gave the CCTV to Scotland Yard for analysis"

This is a dramatization, but close to the dialogue in Red Notice. Does this sound like really bad scenario for a Cops TV series? Browder wants us to believe this is how he was framed. If you think I'm kidding, you will have to read *Red Notice* to find out.

Chapter 12

WHERE DID THE MONEY GO?

BROWDER IS NOW on a mission to find out who was responsible for Magnitsky's death and track down the "blood money" and seek revenge on those who spent the money. Why he cares so much about getting money back into the hands of the Putin government I haven't quite figured out, but let's proceed. This soon becomes so convoluted to anyone trying to keep track of the accusations, for most people, just read his book, it's much simpler.

Over the course of my last two years researching Browder, I have kept a list of everyone he has accused of being complicit in the "blood money". He has a lot of very friendly journalists and financial investigative organizations that will run frequent articles of the latest accused. I will list the articles and save you the trouble of reading the articles and compile a list of all those accused and how much money they were accused of getting in this heist. The articles are in the Bibliography section under the Section listing "those accused of stealing the $230 million from the Russian treasury December 2007". Some of the articles are written by Michael Weiss of The Daily Beast, Luke Harding of The Guardian, and Journalists from the OCCRP, Buzzfeed, and The Telegraph.

From the Russian Federation document submitted to the US Government in the Prevezon case, they state the exact amount was 5.4 billion rubles stolen or $218, 834, 569 US dollars. They claim after Markelov and Khlebnikov were arrested they reclaimed 685, 024,893.29 rubles, so we are left with roughly 4.7 billion with rubles. Let's say roughly $200 million dollars.

So embedded in these articles are phrases like "close associate of Putin's", "Putin's friend", "Putin's cellist", and "Putin's inner circle". You start to see a running theme. Those accused are close to Putin and hate Browder and, again, these are only the accusations I stumbled across. There could be others floating around that I missed.

Victor Yanukovych.	$50 million through a Latvian Bank
Reuben Vardanayn	$130 million through a Lithuanian Bank
Prince Charles	$200,000 used unknowingly on house renovations
Olga Stepanova and ex-husband Vladlen Stepanov	$38 million
Pavel Karpov	Purchased a house and other luxuries
Artem Kuznetsov	Purchased luxuries
Dmitry Klyuev with Associates *	$14 million through Canada, $10 million Switzerland, $40 million through US, and "millions" through France

Igor Sagiryan and V. Dzharbarov	$230 million assisting the "Klyuev gang"
Sergey Roldugin	$800,000
Denis Katsyv	7.6 million in NYC real estate
Pavlo Hrtsyna	$32 million
Alexander Abramov	? Unknown amount
"Tatyana"	16 million euros through paintings in Saint Tropez
Alexander Perepilichny	assisted Stepanovs rinsing $6 million through BVI

……and 50 others Browder requested be added to the sanctions list for being part of theft, cover up or torture of Magnitsky.

I know what you are thinking. I'm making this up right? Well, you can read the articles and see Browder quotes in the articles and decide for yourself.

I also compiled a list of the countries Browder accuses of funneling the money through them in various banks and shell companies. The countries include:

Australia, Latvia, Estonia, Moldova, Switzerland, Russia, Germany, BVI, Cyprus, Belize, Nevis, Lithuania, Ireland, Ukraine, France, Luxembourg, Saint Tropez, Canada, Finland, Austria, and the City of Hong Kong.

What banks? Here's the list.

USB bank (Russia), Intercommerz (Russia), JP Morgan (USA), Deutsche Bank (USA), Wachovia (USA), Citibank (USA), American

Where did the money go?

Express (USA), Danske Bank (Estonian Branch), Mosstoiecombank (Russia), OceanBank (Russia), Pushkin Bank (Russia), Privat Bank (Latvia), Legbank (Ukraine), and UkioBankas (Lithuania)

What companies? Are you ready for this list?

Through Troika Dialog involvement in theft (Reuben Vardanayn)

Reaton Ltd, (BVI), Vantery Union (BVI), Lerwick Holding (BVI), Zarin Group Inc (Belize), Protection Company (BVI), Industrial Trade Corp, Nixford Capital Corp, Quantis Division Ltd

Through KATSYV involvement

000 Rilend, 000 Parfenion, 000 Makhaon, Fausta, ZHK, Anika Univers, Krainly Server, Elenast-com, Zarin Group, Protection Company, Wagtest Limited, Vanteray Union, Robert Transit LLP, Del Networks SA, Arivust Holding LTD, Baikonur Worldwide LTD, Quartell Trading LTD, Nomirec, Bristol Export, Logos Plus, Pluton, Boily systems Ltd

Through Yanukovych

Castlefront LLO (Estonia), Everfront sales LLP (Estonia), Jackwell LLP (Estonia), Unitronic LLP (Estonia), Milltown Corporate Service (BVI), Ireland overseas Acquisitions (BVI), Fineroad Business LLP (UK), Roadfield Capital LLP (UK), Dream Cosmetic, Technomark Busines LTD, Starwell International Ltd, Fynel LTD, Navimax Venture

OCCRP article of 2 Ukranians being involved

Vreston Limited (Cyprus)

Viponix-Snab (Ukraine)

OCCRP article talking about Troika involvement (not included in the Guardian article)

Batherm Venture Ltd (Cyprus)

Matias Ltd (Cyprus)

Dmitry Klyuev partners. Money was funneled into their companies in the UK

Jon Wortley Hunt, company Altem

Andrew Moray Stuart, company Forres Limited

Damian Calderbank, company Kareras Limited

Now, I'm not a numbers person or a financial person by nature, but I look at the various flowcharts and lists of those accused and scratch my head thinking, if all these people were involved in redistributing a mere $200 million amongst each other, then communism is still a thing amongst the elite in Russia. They are certainly dividing their spoils thin.

So, where does Katsyv, that guy Nataliya Veselnitskaya was defending, fit into all this? Wasn't that a really big deal when she met with Trump Jr during the Presidential campaign when she and Rob Goldstone were putting together their devious plan into the subject line of e-mails and holding their secret meeting in a public office building in downtown Manhattan? What was that all about?

It turns out Denis Katsyv was only accused of getting 7.6 million, less than 3% of the haul, but hey, he is the guy Browder will take down for his claims to the "blood money". Katsyv wasn't even put on the sanctions list. The one guy who actually had property in the West got to keep it after the case was settled.

Browder initially went after Renaissance Capital for their involvement in the Hermitage stolen companies, but after Magnitsky died, the US Government switched gears and decided to go after Denis Katsyv and his company, Prevezon for some reason. Nataliya Veselnitskaya represented Prevezon in the case in New York that went on for years. The US government was filing more and more motions, bogging down the system and pressuring Prevezon to plead guilty, hoping they'd cave to stop the bleed of expenses defending themselves. Once Browder testified, the US government realized their case would lose if went to trial. Prevezon and The United States Government agreed to a settlement $ 5.9 million and a not guilty plea by Prevezon and they got to keep their properties.

Chapter 13

BROWDER, VESELNITSKAYA, AND THE DAILY SHOW

WHY DID THE U.S government agree to settle with Russian businessman Denis Katsyv? If you watch the video depositions of Bill Browder and Department of Homeland Security Agent, Todd Hyman, the answer is simple. Their depositions were disasters. Both are posted on YouTube. Browder's deposition is broken into seven, one-hour videos of his seven-hour testimony, and Todd Hyman's is broken into two, one-hour videos. It is clear from Todd Hyman's video that he relied on evidence all submitted by one source, Bill Browder. Other sources that were not in Browder's own words are articles submitted from the OCCRP and Browder friendly journalists, like Michael Weiss, that don't stray far from the Browder narrative. Who gave OCCRP the information? Browder. See how this works?

It was difficult to even get Browder to testify in the U.S courts because he was trying to dodge the subpoenas. His argument was, "They sought to obtain documents about my security, my personal moments, the whistleblowers who helped us, and the law enforcement investigations we assisted. Providing those documents directly to the Russian government would have put me, my family, my colleagues and our community of justice activists in danger of being killed by the Russian government."

The third attempt was successful in issuing the warrant, which involved a foot chase down the snowy streets of New York. Browder was exiting The Daily Show with Jon Stewart after talking about his book on the show. With the new subpoena, Judge Griesa denied Browder's request to not be deposed. Judge Griesa stated, "Apparently the credible threats did not prevent him from going on The Daily Show February 3, Fox and Friends February 3, appearing on Sirius on February 3, going on CNBC Squawk Box on February 3, going on MSNBC on February 5, going on Greg Greenberg's program February 6. Apparently, the threats didn't prevent him from doing that. Now why could he not have been deposed?" With his final ruling on the matter, Judge Griesa explained, "I have reviewed the affidavits and declarations on the issue of whether Browder was properly served with process in New York City. I do not accept the argument that somehow that service of process was ineffective because of some fear of harm from Russian officials. My ruling is that he was served in New York City and properly served." Judge Thomas Griesa ruled on Monday, (March 9 2015) that Mr. William F. Browder must come to New York for a deposition on April 15 to reveal the sources of information he gave to federal prosecutors in the case of United States v Prevezon Holding Ltd.

To get Browder into court took years. Glenn Simpson's company, Fusion GPS, who worked for Prevezon during the case, stated his primary role was getting Browder interviewed. He first tried to subpoena him through his Hermitage Capital Management company that was registered in Delaware, (Hermitage Capital filed documents with the Securities and Exchange Commission) but Browder took his name off and said it was a mistake his name was listed.

Then Glenn got subcontractors to give him the subpoena in Colorado where his ten-million-dollar Aspen home is listed under Tarantino LLC. He also has two cars registered to this address under his name. After Browder spoke at the Aspen Institute in the summer of 2014, Simpson's guys served him a subpoena in the parking lot of the Aspen Institute (putting it on the windshield of his car). Browder dropped it on the ground and drove off towards his mansion, claiming later he thought they were KGB agents. Browder refused the subpoena again when delivered to his home dropping on the doorstep and slamming the door. He argued he wasn't in the United States often enough to serve as a witness. Another time he argued Colorado didn't have jurisdiction over New York. He even argued a conflict of interest issue because one of the lawyers at Baker Hostetler, John Moscow, did work for him. (Yes, that's the lawyers actual name.) This long drawn out battle finally culminated in the April 2015 video deposition hearing.

With Browder finally seated in the deposition chair, there was no make-up or friendly softball questions like he gets on Fox News and CNN. Under oath of swearing to tell the truth is a far different story. Browder even tried to raise his left hand initially to avoid having his statements be legal, but the clerk caught this and asked him to raise his right hand, not his left.

Everyone acts a little differently under oath. Glenn Simpson deposed was honest about what his research into Browder showed, but in Glenn's recent book, he sells a completely different narrative. I was looking forward to reading his book after reading his Senate Judiciary testimony about Browder and was shocked to see Glenn in his book was supporting Browder more, and trying to smear Nataliya Veselnitskaya. It was a disappointing read and I realized the purpose of the book was to continue his Deutsche Bank/Trump opposition research for the 2020 Presidential campaign. This wasn't a book tour like James Comey, Lisa Page, or Andrew McCabe who were trying to polish their image. This was a continuation of the "Deutsche Bank loan given to Trump opposition research", to tie Trump to Russia. Glenn Simpson bought bank statements off the son of a Deutsche Bank CEO. (William Broeksmit, a CEO at Deutsche Bank committed suicide when he was caught up in a corruption scandal at the bank). William Broeksmit's son is Val Broeksmit, who goes by the name @BikiniRobotArmy on Twitter, for the name of his band. He says he sold his dad's papers to Glenn Simpson for $10,000. Val is an interesting follow on Twitter and a hidden player in the Trump/Deutsche Bank smears that may resurface for 2020 Presidential race.

I realized after reading Glenn Simpson's book, a man who probably knew more about Browder's con than most people, as seen by his scathing testimony to the Senate Judiciary Committee, that he had no desire to expose Browder. There just wasn't any political will. Glenn knows the money he can make with smearing Trump is the best cash cow that will pay the mortgage. So "Crime and Progress", written by Co-Founders of Fusion GPS, Glenn Simpson and Peter Fritsch, will do nothing to expose Browder. It will be used to dirty up Trump for 2020 election with Deutsche Bank loan nonsense.

So, with no political will from either side of the aisle in both politics and media, there is not much chance Browder will ever be exposed. The night he was served his subpoena on that snowy street in New York, jumping out of his limo and running down the street, he was not afraid of the KGB, he was running from being forced to tell the truth. The night on the sidewalk outside *The Daily Show* studio set, he was accompanied by Juleanna Glover, not exactly what his Twitter follower crowd would expect from him. Juleanna Glover is a former Republican political strategist and widely considered one of the most powerful lobbyists in Washington D.C. She has her work cut out for her representing Browder. Bill insists she wasn't his lobbyist at the time the subpoena was issued, just his friend. I'm sure Dr. Carpenter, Deputy Assistant Secretary of Defense with the Pentagon, is just a "friend" too when they met at the White House the next week. Probably a big Trevor

Noah and Jon Stewart fan too.

The *Prevezon vs US* case brought a lot of the big guns in lobbying and brought lawyers from Washington D.C to New York City. William Browder hired the law firm of John D. Ashcroft to represent him. Ashcroft is a former Attorney General and Juleanna Glover has worked closely with him for decades. Prevezon, in turn, hired former FBI director, Louis Freeh, to help work on the settlement talks.

When the case first was initiated in the SDNY, Preet Bharara was the U.S attorney for the district. Bharara was replaced by Joon Kim, March 11th, 2017, who was then replaced by Geoffrey Berman January 5th, 2018. The government wanted a legal precedent in the U.S courts to strengthen the Magnitsky Law, but when the evidence given to Congress was deemed inadmissible by Judge Griesa, Browder and the U.S government knew their case had no legal basis.

The case was settled May 2017, with Browder spinning the case as a legal victory for himself and his murdered lawyer. "Justice was served for human rights activists around the world and corrupt Russian oligarchs would now think twice before trying to hide their blood money in America". Nataliya Veselnitskaya was banished to Russia, charged with Obstruction of Justice in the case, and will probably never be allowed to set foot in America again. Her attempts to get her side of the story out were squashed as Browder cheered when her Twitter account was suspended and claimed victory against "Russian trolls". Now with the Prevezon case behind him, Nataliya Veselnitskaya banished from the U.S, Browder could breathe a sigh of relief his Magnitsky Law and story was safe from any scrutiny.

Chapter 14

How did we get here?

How did Sergei Magnitsky allegedly figure out the whole plot as Browder claims? Under oath in 2006, Magnitsky, admits he hadn't talked to Browder in three years, and Browder under oath says he never made attempts to contact Sergei Magnitsky or his lawyers throughout Magnitsky's pre-trial detention from November 2008 until his death eleven months later, November 16th, 2009. So, with no documents anywhere ever unearthed of Browder and Magnitsky communicating, how did Browder and Magnitsky figure out this con? Browder knew there was no documentation anywhere of any correspondence with Magnitsky, so he had to come up with another way he stumbled upon the theft.

This is the part of the book *Red Notice*, and the part of my research that I realized Browder uses the natural deaths of Russians, to spin a narrative favorable to him. Dead men don't talk, so they can't say these secret conversations never happened. Since it's illegal for an average citizen to obtain bank documents and other people's bank records, leaks of "papers" is an invaluable tool for spinning a story. Recently there have been a lot of leaked papers put on websites for anyone to access; yanukovychleaks.org, Panama papers and ICIJ OffShore Leaks Database (International Consortium of Investigative Journalists) are some examples. Organizations like OCCRP (Organized Crime and Corruption Reporting Project) will use these databases and write articles about corruption around the world.

The Panama papers focus on a law firm called Mossack Fonseca and its clients. Netflix did a movie about the law firm called "The Laundromat" starring Meryl Streep as one of the victims to their scams. Antonio Banderas and Gary Oldman were the Mossack Fonseca villains. Funny how the movie doesn't mention Browder's two LLCs managed by Mossack Fonseca, Berkeley Advisers and Starcliff, but I digress.

Vadim Kleiner of Hermitage Capital told The Daily Beast he figured out that former Ukrainian President, Victor Yanukovych, was part of the $230 million tax heist from the Russian government just by reading the Yanukovych leak papers online. Now, grant you, Yanukovych papers were still being fished out of the water and drying across Yanukovych's estate floors using blow-dryers to try to unstick the papers at this time. Yanukovych's evacuation helicopter ride to Russian had barely hit the ground and Kleiner had put together an impressive flow chart tracing $50 million to various Latvian banks in three days simply by checking out the Yanukovych leaks website…right…sure. Why Yanukovych is escaping to a country he supposedly stole $50 million dollars from is never a question asked either.

Billionaires will use these leaks as "evidence" in court against each other when they are fighting for their piece of the pie. It's hard to figure out sometimes, if these are real battles, or they are using these judgements and losses to regain control of companies to avoid paying taxes on documented losses from verdicts. I have no idea which cases are legitimate or not. Take for instance a case with Beny Steinmetz, who was mad at billionaire George Soros for smearing him in his attempts to keep his mining permits on iron ore in the African country Republic of Guinea. Beny was blaming Soros for using his journalists to put negative publicity about him in the papers. George Soros funds OCCRP through his Open Society and until recently, their website listed two financiers, Open Society Foundation and USAid at the bottom of the homepage. Now their website lists a dozen donors in the same Font size, to not pick a favorite. Beny Steinmetz was placed under house arrest December 19th, 2016 but was released one month later without charges. April 2017, His company, BSGR, filed a suit against George Soros in U.S federal court in New York claiming he engaged in a lengthy effort to defame his business using sources like OCCRP. This is a common tactic by Browder and Soros called circular intel, where they will feed a story to a newspaper and then use the newspaper article as a source for their evidence.

None of these attempts were going well for Browder when he used OCCRP as a source in the Prevezon case and he was unable to come up with actual admissible evidence. Prevezon's lawyer kept asking Browder how he knew Katsyv had the "blood money" and Browder would reference power point flow charts. Then Prevezon lawyers asked Department of Homeland Security tax expert, Todd Hyman, the same question. Todd Hyman, one of only three people placed on the Prevezon case by the Department of Homeland Security, was even more of an embarrassment under oath than Browder if that is even possible.

Prevezon lawyer: "Did you get in touch with the banks to see if they were accurate?

Hyman: "No I did not, they were foreign banks."

Prevezon lawyer: "Yeah, does your phone go long distance?"

Hyman: "No it does not"

Prevezon lawyer: "Can you get authority to call or to write abroad?"

Hyman: 'Yes"

Prevezon lawyer: "Did you seek such authority?"

Hyman: "No"

Prevezon lawyer: "Is that true for the entire investigation that no one sought authority to verify with the Russian banks the accuracy of the portions of the records you had?"

Hyman: "Prior to filing the complaint, no"

Todd Hyman's deposition was March 3rd, 2014 and they had yet to seek MLAT with Russian banks. (Mutual Legal Assistance Treaty). The United States froze Denis Katsyv' properties in 2014 based solely on Browder's evidence of flowcharts and copy of bank statements. If no one was able to trace the Russian treasury money into Bristol Export and Nominex (two subsidiaries of Prevazon Holding LLC), there is no case. Browder knows this. The U.S government knows this and Katsyv knows this. They had to come up with a reason to not comply with MLAT and that is political prosecution. The U.S government simply chooses to ignore the evidence given to them from the Katsyv defense and this is perhaps Browder's motivation to forge documents. Rinat Akhmetshin explains at length about the forged documents in his Senate Judiciary testimony.

Under oath, Browder can't explain how they figured out the tracing, but a dead "whistleblower" by the name of Alexander Perepilichny comes in handy in *Red Notice*.

Chapter 15

IS PEREPILICHNY A WHISTLEBLOWER?

ALEXANDER PEREPILICHNY IS a Russian financier who left Russia in 2009 and died while jogging near his $20,000 a month rented home in London. Browder claims Alexander gave the Swiss prosecution documents implicating the Stepanovs, who are part of the "Klyuev Gang", in the Russian tax heist. In a lengthy article written in The Atlantic by Jeffrey Stern, Browder is heavily quoted saying he thinks Alexander Perepilichny was murdered by Russians. Browder's story is so over the top I can't help but chuckle thinking of the journalist, Jeffrey Stern, scribbling in his notebook as Browder proceeds to tell a story that even a credulous ten year old might be skeptical about.

In August 2010, an email came from "Alejandro Sanches" to Browder at Hermitage Capital. Sanches, who turns out to be Perepilichny, decided to come forward because he was so moved by the death of Sergei after watching a YouTube video Browder had posted called the "Untouchables". He states, according to Browder, "Corruption may have become accepted part of doing business in Russia, but killing an innocent man was not okay." One of Browder's lawyers agrees to meet Sanches, whoever he was. The lawyer was accompanied by a four-man security detail. One guard carried a signal jammer. Another did a sweep with a Geiger counter, lest Sanches try to use radioactive poison.

Browder claims the Stepanovs and Perepilichny had a "falling out" and the Stepanovs used their influence to have criminal charges against him and he fled the country. Now he figured if he could shine a light on the Stepanov' crimes, he could hurt their credibility and weaken the case against him. To Browder, Perepilichiny was a criminal plain and simple, but Browder took the bank statements from him anyway. After the first encounter, they meet often and Perepilichny shares documents explaining $6 million of the $38 million the Stepanov' stole was given to him to "rinse" through his shell company in the British Virgin Islands after it first passed through Moldova and Latvia. Perepilichny then passed the money back to the Stepanovs who spent on luxury condos on the man-made island Palm Jumeirah in Dubai.

Browder then made another YouTube video with this new information being careful to protect Perepilichny's identity, but when Vladlen Stepanov watched the video, he saw his condo in the video. He also somehow knew his address was listed in the complaint given to the Swiss, so Stepanov could think of only one person besides himself who knew his Dubai address and it was Perepilichny. Don't ask me how Vladlen Stepanov knew his address is in some Swiss complaint, he just does. It made sense to Browder when he was spinning the story. Don't ask questions, just read Browder's story and go to book club and drink some Chardonnay.

So, Stepanov finds out Perepilichny is snitching on him from a YouTube video. (which is coincidentally also how Perepilichny found out Magnitsky died uncovering the tax heist, cough, cough), Now, according to Browder, his whistleblower is now exposed and must be silenced. So, he is silenced by the "Klyuev Gang" by poisoning him with a Chinese plant he would have to have ingested in Paris before his flight back to London. I know that sounds a bit convoluted, but it's the Russians, they are very clever.

In Jeffrey's lengthy article in *The Atlantic*, a sketched picture of Perepilichny's dead body is stretched out on the ground, with the Chinese plant growing out of his mouth and stomach reaching up into the sky with the Kremlin in the middle of the vines. His mouth gaping open, and squiggly lines are drawn all over him, indicating the poison was throughout his body.

Luke Harding from *The Guardian* also gets in on this story too, saying Perepilichny had been in Paris earlier that morning on the day of his death, having booked two hotels in Paris in different parts of town the night before. That was about all we know about his trip to Paris. Luke claims Perepilichny had met a man in the past who said he was from the Russian government, but he was actually an affiliate of a Russian crime syndicate. It turned out that the affiliate of a Russian crime syndicate was actually Perepilichny's lawyer, Andrey Pavlov. OK, how does Harding know about these interactions and that Perepilichny was duped by a member of the Klyuev Gang posing as a Russian government official? Pavlov told Luke Harding, Perepilichny initiated the meetings, asking for help in determining whether there were any Russian investigations against him. Lawyer Pavlov told Journalist Luke Harding that Alexander Perepilichny knew Pavlov was a lawyer, not a government official. Luke also states Perepilichny had received an ominous phone call informing him that police had found his name on a hit list in the home of an alleged Chechen contract killer. How does Luke Harding know this information three years later? Hmmm, can you think of who his source might be? So, Browder back in 2010 knew this guy fled Russia and there was a Hit list on him, so what does he do? Not mention it for three years? What would you do?

A) Protect this brave whistleblower.

B) Make a YouTube video doxxing your second "whistleblower" that gets him killed by exposing him to the "Klyuev Gang" Oops.

Let's see, how did putting Magnitsky in that first video go? Your first "whistleblower" didn't fair too well after the video. Maybe "Sanches" should have avoided Browder and only went to the UK police with the alleged "hit-list" and not met with Browder so many times. Or maybe Browder just lied to Luke Harding and Luke was happy to be his stenographer.

So, when he had flown back to London that day, Perepilichny arrived home and told his wife he wasn't feeling well and went out for a jog. Soon after, a passerby saw his body on the street and called the police. Two autopsies proved inconclusive, but one of Perepilichny's life insurance companies, Legal and General, ordered tests that detected a toxin from a Chinese flowering plant, Gelemium, in his stomach. The plant was nicknamed "heartbreak grass" because a product in it triggers cardiac arrest if ingested. Mr Perepilichny's other insurers have not raised any objections. Browne, the insurance company lawyer for Legal and General however, even suggested Pavlov should be considered "a candidate for the killing". A British cardiologist employed by the court concluded Perepilichny probably died of natural causes.

Perepilichny's wife fought Browder's effort to try to say he was murdered. Finally, The UK Queen's court in the Perepilichny case noted in their ruling Bill Browder is "rule of media" not "rule of law". There is a similarity in both of the stories of Magnitsky and Perepilichny, that Browder spins a natural death into murder. First, there is no one else claiming murder in both cases except Browder loudly and persistently. The only other person claiming murder in the Perepilichny case was the one life insurance agent, Browne, and that's it. And how does Browne know all about Pavlov to suggest he murdered Perepilichny? I mean, does anyone think Browne was getting his "scoops" from someone with the initials BB? Why does Browder wait three whole years to talk to Luke Harding about all this? If your "whistleblower" got poisoned and you knew he was on a Chechen hitlist, and being duped by "Klyuev Gang members" posing as Government agents, wouldn't you bring it up earlier than three years later? Same as the Magnitsky case. No one mentions a beating except Browder and not until years later. Not even the human rights investigators that explored the case within days of his death mention violence. In both cases Browder makes up a story about the crimes of the "Kyluev Gang" stealing the money, but there isn't one piece of evidence in a paper trail to back up his claims. If he links a piece of paper, it's usually in Russian and the description of what it says is inaccurate. Family members and associates of the deceased dispute his stories. Perepilichny's widow disagreed with him, and even Magnitsky's own mother told Andrei Nekrasov on video she believed her son died of neglect. It's pretty hard to spin a video of an interview with Magnitsky's own mother, but Browder somehow does.

There is a pattern to claiming Russian's murder people and Browder does it so often and in such a reckless way. Like on Twitter when he says Elena Gremina died of a "heart attack". If you Google her picture, and I don't mean to be fresh, but you can see a heart attack isn't that out of the question. Some things just don't add up, like if Perepilichny was claiming Pavlov was a government agent, but he was really part of the Klyuev Gang, wouldn't Perepilichny know this since he was supposedly "coming clean" from being part of the same "Gang" himself? When exactly did Perepilichny figure out Pavlov wasn't in the government? No one really explains this story. It makes absolutely no sense.

How come journalists never ask these questions? Does this dawn on Luke Harding or Michael Weiss or do they just not care because it sells papers. Michael Weiss is the Founding editor of The Interpreter, a site that credits Pavel Khodorkovsky, son of Mikhail Khodorkovsky, in his help for launching the organization. Recently *The Interpreter,* described as "Right wing media" has merged with the media organization funded by the United States government, *Radio Free Europe/Radio Liberty (RFE/RL)* which has been active since the Cold War to combat Soviet Union disinformation. The founder of the Human Rights Foundation, Garry Kasparov, was thankful for Radio Free Europe when he dreamed about Freedom behind the Iron Curtain with only the radio giving him hope. A frequent speaker at these Human Rights campaigns for Kasparov and Browder is Alexey Navalny. Vladlen Stepanov actually sued Alexey Navalny for sharing Browder's YouTube video that smeared Stepanov and Stepanov won the court case of libel in the Russian courts. So that's it. That's the end of my research into "The Magnitsky Hoax." There are a lot of smoking gun hoaxes to choose from in Browder's *Red Notice*. The CCTV video he claims he gave Scotland Yard of the two Eastern European men is one of them. In Browder's book he claims two men were stuffing fake documents from their plastic bag labeled with a logo from a popular retail story in Kazan, Tatarstan into a DHL package in London. The other big smoking gun in his story is the made-up Voicemail from the Blackberry he gave to Scotland Yard. If these events really happened, I just don't understand why he doesn't mention them for years. I mean, if my kid died in prison and his boss had a recording of him being beaten, wouldn't that be the number one thing you'd be screaming about the case from the rooftops? Why isn't this evidence submitted to any human rights group?

Other smoking guns also include Rimma Starova's testimony and Sergei Magnitsky's testimony claiming Eduard M. Khairetdinov was given power of attorney to attend the arbitration court hearings in October 2007. The evidence seems overwhelming and this maybe why when Khairetdinov' offices were raided in August 2008 and the evidence confiscated, Browder needed a way out. I believe Browder most likely came up with the story of the two "Eastern European men" sending the DHL package from London arriving ninety minutes before the police raid to twist being caught. If the "two Eastern European looking men" framed Khairetdinov, why aren't these two guys arrested? You can see the logo of a popular retail store in Tatarstan on the bag they carry with the forged documents incriminating Khairetdinov, but can't identify them? If Scotland Yard couldn't I.D them, why not make public or give to that crackerjack sleuth Eliot Higgins from Bellingcat you give Magnitsky awards to?

In the Luke Harding article and in *Red Notice*, Browder sets up the tale of how Browder and Magnitsky discover the theft like this:

"In 2008, as Browder was trying to launch a new investment fund focused on emerging markets outside of Russia, he got a call from a bailiff in St. Petersburg. The bailiff was asking when the company planned to pay the $71 million judgment it owed. Browder had no idea what the bailiff was talking about, he knew his Moscow office was raided but didn't know how the stolen documents had been used. He asked a tax attorney in Moscow named Sergi Magnitsky to look into it." This scenario is not consistent with Magnitsky's testimony or any other version of events. Browder's version comes with "playing in the pool with his children and his heart pounding before he takes the call from the bailiff". It's filled with emotional stories of him being Putin's enemy number one and being fearful of his life. Browder stated to the Senate Judiciary he received a death threat from the Russian Minister, Dmitry Medvedev, at the World Economic Forum in Davos, Switzerland in 2013. When asked about Magnitsky from a journalist, Medvedev replied, "It's too bad that Sergei Magnitsky is dead and Bill Browder is alive and free." I'm not sure if this an accurate translation of the quote, I would guess Browder made it sound more menacing than the original Russian.

Reading his emotional prose (or Lee Child's) in Red Notice catches a reader, and makes them feel bad if they don't believe him. This can happen to anyone. Maybe this "Klyuev gang" are that clever to have recruited Victor Yanukovych, Sergey Roldugin, the heads of Troika Dialog, Renaissance Capital, and two crooked cops named Karpov and Kuznetsov. Maybe they are that clever to involve over 60 people, 20 countries, 15 banks, and over 50 LLCs, for funneling an amount equaling about $200 million out of Russia. Still, no one can explain why Browder wants to help the Russian government get their money back.

We know the Trump tower meeting was all about Browder because we can see the notes Paul Manafort took on his phone exactly match the deposition of Nataliya Veselnitskaya talking about Browder's cons. This is in public records submitted to the U.S government, so why doesn't a journalist do a quick Google search and figure this out? Do we really think Goldstone was sent by Putin with his devious plot in the subject line of the email and meeting in public?

So, what is this really all about? How can one tax accountant that died in a Russian prison draw the attention of a former U.S attorney general (John Ashcroft) on one side of the court and a former FBI director (Louis Freeh) on the other side of the court? What is really going on here? One can only speculate, as there is so much disinformation out there with the infowars that takes place between the West and Russia.

Chapter 16

Magnitsky's Legacy

So, what is going on here? I think I presented a solid case of questioning the official narrative and showing the glaring contradictions in Bill Browder's book *Red Notice* vs Magnitsky's testimony and others. The underlying question is why are so many powerful people are willing to go along with whatever Browder says? This is the bigger conundrum that can only be answered with speculation. Ask any Senator or CNN reporter about why we should believe Browder and their answer will be as predictable as the sun rising in the East; Putin's regime has a history of disinformation, obfuscation, and outright brazen lies to distort truth. Russia leaves you doubting anything our great intelligence agencies state. Russia creates chaos for chaos sake to destabilize the West so we fight amongst each other. Then, if you are a Democratic Senator or a biased reporter, you will say Trump and Putin use the same tactics, and once again we are fighting amongst our fellow Americans. If you are a Republican Senator or a biased reporter, you will compare Jerry Nadler to Putin. It's a vicious cycle of our own media and politicians polarizing America, then blaming Putin or "the other side" for these frictions, never looking in the mirror themselves. So, what does Browder do? He gets something all media and politicians agree on, "Putin is bad". He takes advantage of the friction between Russia and the West and uses it to hide from his crimes, because it's easy for people to not see both sides of a coin. Bifurcation fallacy of Putin is bad, so Browder must be good, satisfies Congress. For me, there has to be another layer. The simple answer of "politicians are just inept and fooled by Browder" doesn't satisfy me. If you are not conspiratorial, stop at the politicians panned answer, it's probably the right one, but not as fun. Speculation is far more interesting. To reiterate, I'm not taking Russia's side. I have been extremely vocal on Twitter denouncing their brazen accusations that Browder is complicit in five murders. I feel the West will never let Russia extradite Browder, so it's a stalemate as far as him being a pawn in negotiations. In other words, Trump wasn't going to "hand over Browder and McFaul to Putin", despite what screaming Rachel Maddow tells you on MSNBC. Luckily, we are able to get a glimmer into the mind of a certain State Department official in regard to his opinion of Browder. Robert Otto's emails were hacked and put on the internet. Otto's communications show he wasn't buying what Browder was selling. Otto tells John Williams, his boss, at the State Department, "I'm beginning to think we are all part of the Browder PR machine." He also writes to another State Department employee, Nathaniel Reynolds, about a 2011 article published in a Russian newspaper called *"Tomorrow"*. It's written by the editor in chief, Alexander Prokhanov, and is titled "Special Operation". The article was analyzing the $230 million Russian treasury theft and Browder and Magnitsky's role. The article suggests Olga Stepanova, an employee of the Russian tax service for a long time, accused Browder of involvement in the fraudulent schemes. Prokhanov wonders if Browder "did it" and "corrupted it" in "due time". (Referring to the tax office). Otto regards this issue as "sharp" and ponders to Reynolds if Browder was familiar with Stepanova. Bill Browder Bcc'd Otto into a lot of his emails, but the hacked emails that questioned Browder's story I'm sure raised tensions between Otto and Browder. Otto was Bcc'd into the email Browder sent Kyle Parker that was a picture of Veselnitskaya's house. Browder also Bcc'd Otto into the Ken Dillanian emails that pressured Dillanian to scrub his May 2016 story that was critical of Browder. There was another State Department former employee that got heavily involved in running Browder's PR machine. That was Jonathan Winer, Browder's lawyer, and an employee for the PR firm APCO. He sent threatening letters to companies not following Browder's version of events. (Winer/APCO also represent Khodorkovsky's Yukos Oil and their mission to regain their assets from Putin). When a hedge fund manager from Monaco wrote a book critical of Browder, Winer sent a letter to Amazon Books demanding they remove the book from their website. Amazon complied. Krainer, the author, then spent tedious hours cleaning up his book to launch again unto Amazon, only to have it taken down shortly after the second attempt. Blacklisting documentaries, removing books from Amazon, and threatening NBC weren't the only attempts to stop dissenting voices. Browder denied access to one of his most vocal critics, Lucy Komisar, from a speech he gave at Princeton University. I have seen Lucy ask questions at events and she is always professional and articulate with her questions, so she certainly isn't disruptive.

Why is Browder so concerned about keeping such a tight ship on the narrative? Even the title of his book is a lie as Interpol has tweeted out that there is no Red Notice issued on Browder and there never has been. So, who is he? His employee Paul Wrench under oath says he "got kicked out of Russia in 2008", so is the whole "denied entry at the Russia airport in 2005" a lie? In the end, was he just a bagman for some crooked investors in Russia? The Prevezon lawyer talks about how Hermitage was bleeding investors (at least 20%) after 2006 (when the market opened up to buy shares outside of Russia). Did Browder wear out his usefulness and move on to the next country to fleece? Was his Renaissance feud just an act? Were they both caught stealing from the Russian treasury using the same scheme with the same lawyers? In Mikhail Glazunov' book, "*Corporate Strategies in Post Communism Russia*", he describes brilliantly how these schemes were carried out by many companies. Glazunov states "A service of acquisition and holding of Gazprom share for non-residents of the Russian Federation were carried out by many operators of the Russian securities market such as UFG (United Financial Group), Renaissance Capital, Troika Dialog, Alfa-Bank, Aton, Deutsche Bank, Gazprombank, JP Morgan, and many others." Was Och-Ziff Management just being tax cheats? Is that what it boils down to? UFG sells to Deutsche Bank, so we just have billionaires suing billionaires and we are forced spectators to clashes of Titans? So, we now know what Paul Manafort's notes mean on his phone during the Trump Tower meeting. "133m shares" was referring to the illegal purchase of 133 million Gazprom shares by Browder for his primary investors, the Ziff brothers.

Manfort's notes taken on his phone during Trump Tower Meeting

Bill Browder
Offshore-Cyprus
133m shares
Companies
Not invest-loan
Value in Cyprus as inter
Illici
Active sponsors of RNC
Browder hired Joanna Glover
Tied to Cheney
Russian adoption by American families

Now we know why Michael McFaul was put on the Russian's sanction list, along with Browder, Bharara, and Todd Hyman. They were integral players perpetuating the Magnitsky hoax. The hoax is a cover up of the fleecing of billions of capital out of Russia by these companies.

The "Hermitage Effect", as Browder brags is his "activism investment", is not his most talented skill set. Media manipulation is. It has caused Americans that are Democrats and Republicans to point the finger at each other calling each other un-American. Media manipulation is his "Hermitage effect", just like his grandmother's first husband did with being editor of Pravda in Russia. Do you think Democrats will be happy they are defending Dick Cheney with each accolade they bestow Browder at their book clubs? Those that were caught up in the Mueller probe like American citizens, Felix Sater and Carter Page have been called disloyal to America, just by being near Trump. Felix Sater has tweeted out cryptic texts about Browder, like posting the Wikipedia page of Earl Browder with no explanation. Carter Page tweets out "How does Bill Browder know if Russia's a 'dangerous place to do business?' America used to be a safe place until his brand of UK-based 'experts' started telling lies to the media. Did 'lawyer' Magnitsky design Browder's 'grey scheme' Gazprom strategies?" Browder denied knowing who Carter Page was even though he described Page negatively in a tweet six months earlier. Michael McFaul was also "live tweeting" concerns about Carter Page's speech in Russia. Devin Nunes questions McFaul's role in spreading the stories about Carter Page, asking McFaul if he was Michael Isikoff's source for his hit pieces on Carter Page in August 2016. What were Browder and McFaul so concerned about? Browder has smeared both Carter Page and Felix Sater as not loyal to America. This is from a man who renounced his own U.S. citizenship.

The answers are right at our fingertips if we are curious and can move past the partisan fighting that consumes talking heads in American culture. The noise drowns out what is right in front of our eyes. At this point, I feel it's just a waste of time trying to explain this story. It's too convoluted and confusing. Then I get an email from the Human Rights Group that hosted *PutinCon*. They are having another event in New York, this time called The *Oslo Freedom Forum*, and I decide to attend. I want to shake the cynicism that may have made me lose sight of the bigger picture, the crimes of human rights abusers in authoritarian regimes. At a recent Sergei Magnitsky awards ceremony, the co-founder of the *Human Rights Foundation* was given the humanitarian award for his tireless pursuit of activism against tyranny. Other recipients that day were Alexey Navalny for Outstanding Russian Opposition Activist, and Eliot Higgins for Outstanding Investigator journalist. (International).

This time I decide not to do it all in one day and I book a hotel room the size of a closet close to the venue in NYC. It is the recommended hotel so many of the attendees and speakers are staying at the hotel. The next day I head down to the conference held at Lincoln Hall. It is similar to *PutinCon* with Its flashy set up in the lobby. The *Oslo Freedom Forum* event has vendors from companies showing their products to activists and attendees gathered around. A company called Consensys is selling Ethereum blockchain and pursuing joint ventures with companies called Sentry and Hala Systems. Sentry is a threat prediction system that resulted in a 20-27% reduction in casualty rates in several areas of Syria under heavy bombardment. There is a cartoon picture of a warplane and a computer and I don't understand the correlation between Ethereum and locally administrable knowledge platforms in warzones, so I move on to the next booth. The company is Afari and the spokesperson explains its mission. He says Afari is a decentralized social network that gives people more privacy and control over their data and who can access. He's saying it's good for protestors in authoritarian governments to be able to coordinate away from lurking government spying. He says he used to sell blockchain encryption, but recently joined Afari because data privacy is the future. I move on to the expansive Fashion and Art area with a poster explaining how Authoritarian regimes regularly harass, jail, and even kill artists because they know how powerful the creative arts can be in challenging tyranny. There is a list of the Václav Havel International Prize recipients for creative dissent. Pussy Riot, the Russian punk rock band, won this award in 2014. Other artist recipients are from all over the world including China, Bahrain, Iran, Cuba, Venezuela, North Korea, and Tibet. The Fashion section of the exhibit is clothing worn in protests. There is the "Orange t-shirt", the color the opposition demonstrators wore protesting Victor Yanukovych's regime and his connection to Russia. The Fashion display is called "Wear Your Values", and the Human Rights Foundation is partnering with an organization "Remake", to facilitate collaborations between activists and designers to highlight the power of fashion as a tool for expression, advocacy, and activism. I chat with attendees. I talk to a nineteen-year-old college dropout who has his own start up for Privacy Technologies for Home or Business. He got a free ticket from Peter Thiel to attend. He says he's financed by Peter Thiel who recruited him from college, and he hands me his card, "*None of Your Business is Our Business.*" I want to ask him if he got four million in seed money like Peter Thiel gave Joshua Browder for his start up app, but I didn't want to crush his dreams, so I stayed quiet. I chat with a middle-aged woman from Brooklyn who is talking about a recent book signing she went to by an Egyptian author called "*F**k the Patriarchy*". I talk to Nicholas from Rwanda, who is at Colombia University for the semester living at the International House, a non-profit residence. He says his program gave him free tickets to attend Oslo Freedom Forum, so he walked over. I also ran into a journalist from The Washington Free Beacon I had lunch with at PutinCon and we agreed to have lunch together again at break. Oslo Freedom Forum and The Human Rights Foundation are organizations run by Thor Halvorssen and Garry Kasparov who put on programs throughout the world for human rights campaigners. Thor talked about former speakers at Oslo Freedom Forum that have been killed recently; Jamal Khashoggi, Raed Fares, and the near miss of Arkady Babchenko, but he outsmarted his would-be assassins by faking his own assassination and smoking out the planners. He covered himself in pig's blood and sent out a picture of his body face down on the ground. He shows up at the press conference talking about his murder, much to the surprise of his wife. I saw Arkady speak at *PutinCon*, and I can't picture this serious man acting out his own death, it was an eerie thought.

Thor then sits down with Enes Kanter, an NBA basketball player from Turkey, now banned from Turkey after he sent out a Facebook post comparing Erdogan to Golum from Lord of the Rings in side by side pictures. Enes talks about his positive experiences in the Gülen schools in Turkey and says he was with Fethullah Gülen the night of the coup attempt on Erdogan. Erdogan blames the coup attempt on Gülen. Enes flashes a smile to Thor and ensures him he was not part of the plot to take out the Turkish government. Each speakers' segment is about fifteen minutes long, with music and slides for their introduction unto the stage, similar to the TED talks you see on YouTube.

We then have a North Korean woman who escaped through Mongolia who spent a lot of her time on stage trashing Trump; a Chinese man with no legs who was run over by a tank in Tiananmen square during the 1989 uprising; and a comedian, Joanne Hausman, who escaped Venezuela but forgets to disclose to the audience her dad is head of InterAmerica Development Bank and a fierce opponent to Maduro. At this point my cynicism is ramping up and I feel like I am at a regime change CIA day camp.

I am empathetic to all the speakers' experiences and do not want to minimize any of their suffering and pain. It is when the young girl from Afghanistan speaks that I become emotional. The U.S State Department worked to get her robotic team's visas to an international competition and she and her teammates ended up winning. Her dad had always been supportive of her pursuing her dreams in science, despite heavy pressure in her country for woman to be silenced. A week after she returned home from winning the competition, her father was taken by ISIS and killed. Her describing the event was one of the most heart wrenching stories I had ever heard and as we gave her a standing ovation, the tears streamed down by cheeks without being wiped away.

I wanted to run on the stage and hug her and tell her to go home and hide and stay away from all of these speaking gigs. I could never ever fathom what she has lived through; me living in Freedom and her under tyranny. This is how the world is divided by HRF, black and white, literally in their brochures. I can still picture this demure Afghan girl in her oversized glasses speaking in her native tongue while the interpreter translates her beautiful prose through my headphones. The translation was very poetic, and I'm sure was not doing justice to the original Pashto. Her story will stay with me for the rest of my life and I will never forget her. After the event I drive home to Boston knowing I can hug my family and I feel so blessed and so grateful to not have my own human rights tragedy to tell. The tears stream from my eyes again as I hold the steering wheel, lost in my thoughts on the speakers' stories.

I have the urge to meet Sergei Magnitsky's family and hug his mother, his wife, and his kids. I want to tell them their son, their husband, and their dad did matter. That is the big picture in all of this. We should not spend our time divided. We read best sellers on either side of the aisle hating Trump, loving Trump, or hating Putin, loving Navalny. Maybe we need to realize using everyday humans as political footballs is not the answer. Maybe having Magnitsky's name on a law weakens his legacy, his legacy of just being a dad who loved his kids, loved his wife, and loved his mom. He wasn't a Saint and he wasn't the Devil. He was a tax accountant that got arrested for a crime and died in pre-trial detention from medical ineptness. That is enough of a story. He should be able to Rest in Peace. Mystery solved.

Epilogue

THE HERMITAGE EFFECT: BUYING LARGE SHARES OF COMMODITIES IN AUTHORITARIAN REGIME COUNTRIES AND THEN THROWING IN A SLICE OF CONDEMNATION FOR A COUNTRY'S HUMAN RIGHTS ABUSES TO EASE THE SOUL.

In anticipation of the Russian market opening up to outside investors, Browder divested from Russia in 2005 and in 2006 began investing in new markets, especially in the Middle East. Browder's Russian bank accounts weren't empty because he was "kicked out" of Russian in 2005, they were practically empty because this was the time period Gazprom shares became available to foreign buyers, leaving a bagman like Browder useless.

Browder was traveling extensively in 2006, and heavily investing in the Middle East, especially in the United Arab Emirates and Saudi Arabia. About two thirds of Hermitage Capital Management's private equity portfolio was invested in the Middle East, including the UAE, Saudi Arabia, Qatar, and Kuwait in 2006. As Browder stated at the time, "The region is profiting from oil wealth transfer and you can just feel it on the ground."

The website "Institution Investor", run by Sheikh Al Qassemi was very complimentary of Browder. Sheikh Sultan bin Sood Al Qassemi praised The Hermitage Fund's arrival saying it was "welcome for new GCC markets". Browder was also singing the praises of UAE- based firms such as ALDAR, which he labelled in 2008 as "one of the cleanest, clearest stories I have ever seen" at a major investors conference in New York. One of the main things that attracted him to the Gulf was the market crash of 2005 stating "the best time to buy is after a crash."

Sheik Al Qassemi is the chairman of Barjeel Securities in the UAE and was a vocal voice on Twitter during the Arab Spring and named in the top 100 Twitter feeds in 2011 in the world. In February 2014, he was ranked 63rd in the "Most Powerful Arabs in Gulf Business" list. Barjeel Geojit Securities is located on Khalid Bin Waleed Road in Dubai. Browder also invested heavily in the Dubai based fertilizer company, Gubre Fabrikalari TAS, under his company, Hermitage Global Master.

Steve Bryant wrote In February 23, 2011, in the Turkish newspaper, Miliyet, stating Dubai based businesses were setting up branches in Turkey to trade more easily with Iran, citing Mehmet Kocaman, the Turkish part owner of an Iranian fertilizer market. Kocaman said his company Gŭbre Fabrikalari TAS had been approached for advice on how to make transfers to and from Iran despite the banking restrictions sparked by U.S sanctions over Iran's nuclear program. He didn't name the companies. Gŭbre Fabrikalari, known as Gubretas, plans additional investments at its Iranian plant to add 1 million tons of new capacity, Milliyet said, citing Kocaman.

Recently, Bill Browder has been heavily tweeting about Human Right Abusers in Saudi Arabia, Iran, and other Middle Eastern countries. The SALT convention, run by Anthony Scaramucci, will be held in The United Arab Emirates this year. Unclear if Bill Browder or Michael McFaul are scheduled to attend.

Bibliography

Books

COOLEY, ALEXANDER A. *DICTATORS WITHOUT BORDERS: Power and Money in Central Asia.* YALE University Press, 2019.

Simpson, Glenn R., and Peter Fritsch. *Crime in Progress: inside the Steele Dossier and the Fusion GPS Investigation of Donald Trump.* Random House, 2019. (64)

Browder, Bill. *Red Notice: How I Became Putin's No. 1 Enemy.* Simon and Schuster Books, 2016. (19, Page 63), (50 Page 276-277)

McFaul, Michael. *From Cold War to Hot Peace: the inside Story of Russia and America.* Penguin Books, 2019. (54- pages 364-371)

Klehr, Harvey, et al. *The Secret World of American Communism.* Yale University Press, 1996.

Websites

Lucy, Komisar. "The Man behind the Magnitsky Act." *Thekomisarscoop.com*, www.thekomisarscoop.com/. (14)

"Browder's War with Sidanco." *Jimmysllama*, 2 Nov. 2017,

jimmysllama.com/. (11) (23)

"J'Accuse News - The Magnitsky Myth & Other Keys to the Geopolitical Hoax of the Century." *J'Accuse News - The Magnitsky Myth & Other Keys to the Geopolitical Hoax of the Century*, jaccuse. news/.

Lee, and John Gensler. "DHS Todd Hyman Deposition." *Populist. TV*, 16 May 2019, thepopulist.us/.

Magnitsky Ru, usa-s. "Proposed List of 60 Russians Browder Requests for Sanctions." *Issuu*, issuu.com/usa-s/docs/magnitsky. (41) (48)

"US STATE DEPARTMENT OFFICIAL ROBERT OTTO GOT HACKED." *English News Front*, 13 July 2017, en.news-front. info/2017/07/14/us-state-department-official-robert-otto-got-hacked/. (72)

DEPOSITIONS, GOVERNMENT EXECUTIVE ORDERS, REPORTS, AND MAGNITSKY NOTES

"Executive Order Blocking the Property of Persons Involved in Serious Human Rights Abuse or Corruption." *The White House*, The United States Government, www.whitehouse.gov/presidential-actions/executive-order-blocking-property-persons-involved-serious-human-rights-abuse-corruption/. (4)

"Senate Judiciary Committee Interview of Glenn Simpson/By Mr. Davis (1)." *Senate Judiciary Committee Interview of Glenn Simpson/ By Mr. Davis (1) - Wikisource, the Free Online Library*, en.wikisource. org/wiki/Senate_Judiciary_Committee_Interview_of_Glenn_Simpson/ By_Mr._Davis_(1). (20) (21)

Sergei Magnitsky's Testimony June 2006, June 2008, and October 2008. (31) (39) (40)

Rimma Starova testimony *https://www.thekomisarscoop.com/wp-content/uploads/2019/05/Starova-Testimony-10-July-08-1.pdf* (38) (60)

25 Handwritten notes from Butyrka prison between July 26th 2008 and September 2009 *http://russian-untouchables.com/docs/D107.pdf* Articles (42) Public Oversight Committee report submitted to the Wall Street Journal *http://online.wsj.com/public/resources/documents/WSJ-20091229-MagnitskyReport.pdf*. (43)

Physicians for Human Rights report Cambridge MA *https://s3.amazonaws.com/PHR_Reports/magnitsky-report-july2011.pdf* (44)

"May 21st Nightly Press Traffic Summary . Bloomberg Article Scrubbed Linking Hillary to Russian with Renaissance Capital $500,00 WJC Speech." *WikiLeaks*, wikileaks.org/podesta-emails/emailid/303. (55)

Articles

"Moscow Accuses Bill Browder of Poisoning Sergey Magnitsky, as Russia Is Expected to Win Interpol's next Presidency." *Meduza*, meduza.io/en/feature/2018/11/19/moscow-accuses-bill-browder-of-poisoning-sergey-magnitsky-as-russia-is-expected-to-win-interpol-s-next-presidency. (1)

Deutsche Welle. "Kremlin Critic Alexei Navalny Says He Was Poisoned in Custody: DW: 02.08.2019." *DW.COM*, www.dw.com/en/kremlin-critic-alexei-navalny-says-he-was-poisoned-in-custody/a-49856462. (3)

Gray, Rosie. "Bill Browder's Testimony to the Senate Judiciary Committee." *The Atlantic*, Atlantic Media Company, 26 July 2017, www.theatlantic.com/politics/archive/2017/07/bill-browders-testimony-to-the-senate-judiciary-committee/534864/. (5) (6)

Hines, Nico. "GOP Lawmaker Got Direction From Moscow, Took

It Back to D.C." *The Daily Beast*, The Daily Beast Company, 19 July 2017, www.thedailybeast.com/gop-lawmaker-got-direction-from-moscow-took-it-back-to-dc. (8)

Brenner, Marie. "Inside Bill Browder's War Against Putin." *Vanity Fair*, Vanity Fair, 3 Jan. 2019, www.vanityfair.com/news/2018/11/bill-browder-war-against-putin. (10)

Bloomberg.com, Bloomberg, www.bloomberg.com/news/articles/2018-07-30/russian-court-rejects-hsbc-settlement-deal-in-browder-case. (12)

Matthews, Owen. "Hoping For A Gusher." *Newsweek*, Newsweek, 14 Mar. 2010, www.newsweek.com/hoping-gusher-108213. (15) Article talking about how in 2006 shares opened up to outside of Russia companies

McClenaghan, Maeve. "Putin and the $100 Million Deal That Disappeared." *The Bureau of Investigative Journalism*, The Bureau of Investigative Journalism, 12 Nov. 2019, www.thebureauinvestigates.com/stories/2012-04-19/putin-and-the-100-million-deal-that-disappeared. (22)

Ames, Mark. "Neocons 2.0: The Problem with Peter Pomerantsev." *Pando*, 18 May 2015, pando.com/2015/05/17/neocons-2-0-the-problem-with-peter-pomerantsev/. Browder Quotes (16)

McCormick, Jason. "5 Citizens Who Left the U.S. to Avoid Paying Tax." *CBS News*, CBS Interactive, 11 July 2012, www.cbsnews.com/media/5-citizens-who-left-the-us-to-avoid-paying-tax/. (17)

Kravtsova, Yekaterina. "Witnesses in Magnitsky Trial Questioned Over Illegal Tax Breaks." *The Moscow Times*, The Moscow Times, 8 Jan. 2020, www.themoscowtimes.com/2013/04/21/witnesses-in-magnitsky-trial-questioned-over-illegal-tax-breaks-a23450. (25)

The Moscow Times. "Artyom Chaika Added to U.S. Magnitsky List for Alleged Corruption." *The Moscow Times*, The Moscow Times, 8 Jan. 2020, www.themoscowtimes.com/2017/12/22/artyom-chaika-added-to-us-magnitsky-list-for-alleged-corruption-a60021. (28)

"Interview of Zoya Svetova." *"Они Банально Перестарались": Зоя Светова - о Гибели Сергея Магнитского - Открытая Россия*, openrussia.org/post/view/929/. (29)

Spiegel, Der. "SPIEGEL Responds to Browder Criticisms of Magnitsky Story - DER SPIEGEL - International." *DER SPIEGEL*, DER SPIEGEL, 17 Dec. 2019, www.spiegel.de/international/world/spiegel-responds-to-browder-criticisms-of-magnitsky-story-a-1301716.html#ref=rss. (30)

Nekrasov, Andre. "Bill Browder and His Story about the Alleged Whistleblower Sergei Magnitsky." *The Magnitsky Act - Behind the Scenes*, magnitskyact.com/telepolis. (32)

Lakic, Vanja. "U.S. Traces US$7.5 Million from Russian Fraud Scheme Uncovered by Magnitsky." *Organized Crime and Corruption Reporting Project*, www.occrp.org/en/daily/6342-u-s-traces-us-7-5-million-from-russian-fraud-scheme-uncovered-by-magnitsky. (34)

Weiss, Michael. "Moscow's Long, Corrupt Money Trail." *The Daily Beast*, The Daily Beast Company, 22 Mar. 2014, www.thedailybeast.com/moscows-long-corrupt-money-trail. (35)

Subscribe to the FT to Read: Financial Times Hermitage in Russian Fraud Claim." *Subscribe to Read | Financial Times*, Financial Times, www.ft.com/content/da0bbffe-01b7-11dd-a323-000077b07658. (36)

"Kommersant. Kamea Charges on Browder and Cherkasov" April 3, 2008 in Kommersant Newspaper." *МВД Ищет Инвестора – Газета Коммерсантъ № 55 (3872) От 03.04.2008*, Газета "Коммерсантъ" №55 От 03.04.2008, Стр.

1, 2 Apr. 2008, www.kommersant.ru/doc/875770. (37)

Perepilichny poisoning Story by Jeffrey E. Stern. "An Enemy of the Kremlin Dies in London." *The Atlantic*, Atlantic Media Company, 3 Jan. 2017, www.theatlantic.com/magazine/archive/2017/01/the-poison-flower/508736/. (66)

Harding, Luke, and Shaun Walker. "'Poisoned' Russian Whistleblower Was Fatalistic over Death Threats." *The Guardian*, Guardian News and Media, 19 May 2015, www.theguardian.com/uk-news/2015/may/19/poisoned-russian-whistleblower-was-fatalistic-over-death-threats. (68)

Wright, Dan. "US State Media Merges With Right Wing Interpreter Mag." *Shadowproof*, 5 Jan. 2016, shadowproof.com/2016/01/05/us-state-media-merges-with-right-wing-interpreter-mag/. Article about Michael Weiss's Mag merging with RFE/RL (70)

Milliyet.com.tr. "ABD Ambargosundan Kaçan Türkiye'ye Geliyor." *Milliyet*, Milliyet, 22 Feb. 2011, www.milliyet.com.tr/ekonomi/abd-ambargosundan-kacan-turkiye-ye-geliyor-1355889.

VIDEOS

Browder, Laura. "'Communism Is Twentieth Centruy Americanism.'" *YouTube*, YouTube, www.youtube.com/watch?v=AXBamA7M22A&list=PLBueTooglw14j36r_wQS4jXMmsWIglkyh&index=8&t=0s. (9)

Untouchable video 2 https://www.youtube.com/watch?v=ok6ljV-WfRw. (33)

Browder, Bill. "Stanford Speech at His 20th Year Reunion, Less than One Month before Magnitsky's Death." *YouTube*, YouTube, www.youtube.com/watch?v=84MsRuC-1l8. (13)

"Browder Deposition Part 1 in Prevezon vs U.S Case

Apirl 2015." *YouTube*, YouTube, www.youtube.com/watch?v=pu9DMxfTGhY&t=1s. (18)

"Interviews of Disabled 'Offshore People' in Kalmykia." *YouTube*, YouTube, www.youtube.com/watch?v=6_E-OyTb3zk. (26)

"Browder and Kara Murza at University of Chicago 2019." *YouTube*, YouTube, www.youtube.com/watch?v=Ux51Bqc3Un0. (52)

Tweets

Mouradian, Regina "But in RFs Defense I Don't Think They Murdered Elena Gremina, Perepilichny, Magnitsky, or the Other Dozen People Browder Says They Did. (Or STRONGLY IMPLIES) Pic.twitter.com/0PaKTf1BxE." *Twitter*, Twitter, 27 Sept. 2019, twitter.com/Justafool2764/status/1177372487484694529?s=20. (2)

Mouradian, Regina Picture of altered report from "special means were" to "a rubber baton was" https://twitter.com/Justafool2764/status/1120403876425936896/photo/1Films (45)

https://twitter.com/carterwpage/status/1126416231467241472?s=20. Tweet on Browder

https://twitter.com/felixsater/status/1165800952126947330?s=20. Felix Sater tweet on Earl Browder

https://threadreaderapp.com/thread/1024398525138968577.html. Copy of documents submitted to Prevezon case from Katsyv lawyers

Dyrekilde, Birgitte https://twitter.com/BDyrekilde/status/1131249573677142021?s=20

https://twitter.com/jimmysllama/status/1165717007637131264?s=20

Links to Articles that Accuse people of being involved in the $230 million stolen from the Russian treasury December 2007

Bobbo, and Eric Kovalsky. "Bill Browder and the Russian Attorney." *Jimmysllama*, 13 Mar. 2019, jimmysllama.com/2017/07/13/10127/.

Cardin, Ben. "Russians Banned under Magnitsky Act." *Russian's Sanctioned*, www.russian-untouchables.com/docs/D71-Final_list_visa_ban_0426101.pdf.

Garside, Juliette, and Caelainn Barr. "Banking Leak Exposes Russian Network with Link to Prince Charles." *The Guardian*, Guardian News and Media, 4 Mar. 2019, www.theguardian.com/world/2019/mar/04/banking-leak-exposes-russian-network-link-to-prince-charles-troika-laundromat.

Garside, Juliette, and Caelainn Barr. "Banking Leak Exposes Russian Network with Link to Prince Charles." *The Guardian*, Guardian News and Media, 4 Mar. 2019, www.theguardian.com/world/2019/mar/04/banking-leak-exposes-russian-network-link-to-prince-charles-troika-laundromat.

Gray, Rosie. "Companies Linked To Ousted Ukrainian President Connected To Magnitsky Investigation." *BuzzFeed News*, BuzzFeed News, 26 Feb. 2014, www.buzzfeednews.com/article/rosiegray/companies-linked-to-ousted-ukrainian-president-connected-to.

Hermitage. "The Hermitage Case: Organized Crime and Legal Nihilism Inside the Russian Government." *Hermitage Website*, Mar. 2009, wikileaks.org/gifiles/attach/172/172317_Hermitage%20Presentation.pdf.

IRPI, OCCRP and. "Bank Records Link President of Cyprus to 'Troika Laundromat'." *OCCRP*, www.occrp.org/en/troikalaundromat/bank-records-link-president-of-cyprus-to-troika-laundromat.

"Law and Order in Russia, The Story behind the Largest Tax Fraud in Russian History." *Law and Order in Russia RSS*, 27 Oct. 2016, lawandorderinrussia.org/2016/us-14-million-connected-to-proceeds-of-us-230-million-fraud-uncovered-by-magnitsky-have-been-traced-to-canada/.

Loginova, Elena. "Money from 'Magnitsky Case' Passed Through Ukraine." *Organized Crime and Corruption Reporting Project*, www.occrp.org/en/daily/8399-money-from-magnitsky-case-passed-through-ukraine.

Mikhailov, Semen. "The Magnitsky Affair Reached St Tropez." *.Ru*, 25 June 2015, www.gazeta.ru/business/2015/06/25/6853957.shtml.

Sawer, Robert Mendick; Patrick. "Russian Crimelord Accused of 'Orgy of Spending' in UK." *The Telegraph*, Telegraph Media Group, 3 May 2016, www.telegraph.co.uk/news/2016/05/03/russian-crimelord-accused-of-orgy-of-spending-in-uk/.

"Stop the Untouchables. Justice for Sergei Magnitsky." *Stop the Untouchables Justice for Sergei Magnitsky UK Companies Accused of Money Laundering in Magnitsky Probe Comments, www.russian-untouchables.com/eng/2013/04/uk-companies-accused-of-money-laundering-in-magnitsky-probe/#more-8942*. Money laundered in Australia *https://www.youtube.com/watch?v=yVsqJ8XQ7mw&feature=youtu.be*

Notes

1. "Moscow Accuses Bill Browder of Poisoning Sergey Magnitsky, as Russia Is Expected to Win Interpol's next Presidency." *Meduza*, meduza.io/en/feature/2018/11/19/moscow-accuses-bill-browder-of-poisoning-sergey-magnitsky-as-russia-is-expected-to-win-interpol-s-next-presidency. (1) https://twitter.com/Justafool2764/status/1177372487484694529?s=20

2. Deutsche Welle. "Kremlin Critic Alexei Navalny Says He Was Poisoned in Custody: DW: 02.08.2019." *DW.COM*, www.dw.com/en/kremlin-critic-alexei-navalny-says-he-was-poisoned-in-custody/a-49856462. (3)

3. "Executive Order Blocking the Property of Persons Involved in Serious Human Rights Abuse or Corruption." *The White House*, The United States Government, www.whitehouse.gov/presidential-actions/executive-order-blocking-property-persons-involved-serious-human-rights-abuse-corruption/. (4)

4. Gray, Rosie. "Bill Browder's Testimony to the Senate Judiciary Committee." *The Atlantic*, Atlantic Media Company, 26 July 2017, www.theatlantic.com/politics/archive/2017/07/bill-browders-testimony-to-the-senate-judiciary-committee/534864/. (5) (6)

5. Ibid

6. Ibid

7. Hines, Nico. "GOP Lawmaker Got Direction From Moscow, Took It Back to D.C." *The Daily Beast*, The Daily Beast Company, 19 July 2017, www.thedailybeast.com/gop-lawmaker-got-direction-from-moscow-took-it-back-to-dc. (8)

8. Browder, Laura. "'Communism Is Twentieth Centruy Americanism.'" *YouTube*, YouTube, www.youtube.com/watch?v=AXBamA7M22A&list=PLBueTooglw14j36r_wQS4jXMmsWIglkyh&index=8&t=0s. (9)

9. Brenner, Marie. "Inside Bill Browder's War Against Putin." *Vanity Fair*, Vanity Fair, 3 Jan. 2019, www.vanityfair.com/news/2018/11/bill-browder-war-against-putin. (10)

10. "Browder's War with Sidanco." *Jimmysllama*, 2 Nov. 2017, jimmysllama.com/. (11)

11. (23)*Bloomberg.com*, Bloomberg, www.bloomberg.com/news/articles/2018-07-30/russian-court-rejects-hsbc-settlement-deal-in-browder-case.

12. Browder, Bill. "Stanford Speech at His 20th Year Reunion, Less than One Month before Magnitsky's Death." *YouTube*, YouTube, www.youtube.com/watch?v=84MsRuC-1l8. (13)

13. Komisar, Lucy "The Man behind the Magnitsky Act." *Thekomisarscoop.com*, www.thekomisarscoop.com/. (14)

14. Matthews, Owen. "Hoping For A Gusher." *Newsweek*, Newsweek, 14 Mar. 2010, www.newsweek.com/hoping-gusher-108213. (15) Article talking about how in 2006 shares opened up to outside of Russia companies

Notes

15. Ames, Mark. "Neocons 2.0: The Problem with Peter Pomerantsev." *Pando*, 18 May 2015, pando.com/2015/05/17/neocons-2-0-the-problem-with-peter-pomerantsev/. Browder Quotes (16)

16. McCormick, Jason. "5 Citizens Who Left the U.S. to Avoid Paying Tax." *CBS News*, CBS Interactive, 11 July 2012, www.cbsnews.com/media/5-citizens-who-left-the-us-to-avoid-paying-tax/. (17)

17. "Browder Deposition Part 1 in Prevezon vs U.S Case Apirl 2015." *YouTube*, YouTube, www.youtube.com/watch?v=pu9DMxfTGhY&t=1s. (18)Browder, Bill. Red Notice: How I Became Putin's No. 1 Enemy. Simon and Schuster Books, 2016. (19, Page 63) Browder, Bill. *Red Notice: How I Became Putin's No. 1 Enemy*. Simon and Schuster Books, 2016. (Page 63),

18. Simpson, Glenn https://en.wikisource.org/wiki/Senate_Judiciary_Committee_Interview_of_Glenn_Simpson/By_Mr._Davis_(1)

19. Idib

20. McClenaghan, Maeve. "Putin and the $100 Million Deal That Disappeared." *The Bureau of Investigative Journalism*, The Bureau of Investigative Journalism, 12 Nov. 2019, www.thebureauinvestigates.com/stories/2012-04-19/putin-and-the-100-million-deal-that-disappeared

21. "Browder's War with Sidanco." *Jimmysllama*, 2 Nov. 2017, jimmysllama.com/. (11) (23

22. Andrew Wood was adviser to Dmitry Prokhorov from Renaissance Capital. Also Wood was the one who told John McCain about the "Dirty Dossier"

23. Kravtsova, Yekaterina. "Witnesses in Magnitsky Trial Questioned Over Illegal Tax Breaks." *The Moscow Times*, The Moscow Times, 8 Jan. 2020, www.themoscowtimes.com/2013/04/21/witnesses-in-magnitsky-trial-questioned-over-illegal-tax-breaks-a23450. (25)

24. "Interviews of Disabled 'Offshore People' in Kalmykia." *YouTube*, YouTube, www.youtube.com/watch?v=6_E-OyTb3zk. (26)

25. Ibid

26. Kravtsova, Yekaterina. "Witnesses in Magnitsky Trial Questioned Over Illegal Tax Breaks." *The Moscow Times*, The Moscow Times, 8 Jan. 2020, www.themoscowtimes.com/2013/04/21/witnesses-in-magnitsky-trial-questioned-over-illegal-tax-breaks-a23450.

27. Zoya, Svetova. "'Они Банально Перестарались': Зоя Светова - о Гибели Сергея Магнитского ." *"Они Банально Перестарались": Зоя Светова - о Гибели Сергея Магнитского - Открытая Россия*, openrussia.org/post/view/929/.

28. Spiegel, Der. "SPIEGEL Responds to Browder Criticisms of Magnitsky Story - DER SPIEGEL - International." *DER SPIEGEL*, DER SPIEGEL, 17 Dec. 2019, www.spiegel.de/international/world/spiegel-responds-to-browder-criticisms-of-magnitsky-story-a-1301716.html#ref=rss. (30)

29. Magnitsky, Sergei 1https://100r.org/media/2017/10/Magnitsky-Testimonies-Oct-2006-June-2008-Oct-2008.pdf English translations of his October 2006, June 2008, and October 2008 testimony

30. Nekrasov, Andrei. "After Vimeo's Succumbing to Another of Browder's Endless Gagging Assaults 'The Magnitsky Act..' Film Is Online Again! On a Website Helping Viewers thru

Context. Pls Share to Debunk the Mega Hoax Washing Gullible Brains & Bailing out White Collar Gangsters!Https://T.co/FbO71TUDh9." *Twitter*, Twitter, 21 Sept. 2018, twitter.com/antiputinismus/status/1043161780543995904.

31. Untouchable video 2 https://www.youtube.com/watch?v=ok6ljV-WfRw. (33)

32. Lakic, Vanja. "U.S. Traces US$7.5 Million from Russian Fraud Scheme Uncovered by Magnitsky." *Organized Crime and Corruption Reporting Project*, www.occrp.org/en/daily/6342-u-s-traces-us-7-5-million-from-russian-fraud-scheme-uncovered-by-magnitsky.

33. Weiss, Michael. "Moscow's Long, Corrupt Money Trail." *The Daily Beast*, The Daily Beast Company, 22 Mar. 2014, www.thedailybeast.com/moscows-long-corrupt-money-trail. (35)

34. Belton, Catherine. Financial Times Hermitage in Russian Fraud Claim." *Subscribe to Read | Financial Times*, Financial Times, www.ft.com/content/da0bbffe-01b7-11dd-a323-000077b07658. (36) As a side note I can't help but notice this article in the Financial Times was written by Catherine Belton, a Moscow based journalist who wrote a hit piece on Sergei Millian during the beginnings of RussiaGate.

35. "Kommersant. Kamea Charges on Browder and Cherkasov" April 3, 2008 in Kommersant Newspaper." *МВД Ищет Инвестора – Газета Коммерсантъ № 55 (3872) От 03.04.2008*, Газета "Коммерсантъ" №55 От 03.04.2008, Стр. 1, 2 Apr. 2008, www.kommersant.ru/doc/875770. (37)

36. Starova, Rimma https://www.thekomisarscoop.com/wp-content/uploads/2019/05/Starova-Testimony-10-July-08-1.pdf.

Translation of Rimma Starova police interview April 9th 2008

37. Magnitsky, Sergei https://100r.org/media/2017/10/Magnitsky-Testimonies-Oct-2006-June-2008-Oct-2008.pdf Magnitsky June 2008. (Scroll past the 2006 page, also contains the October 2008)

38. Ibid

39. Proposed Magnitsky List https://issuu.com/usa-s/docs/magnitsky List of submission of alleged candidates

40. Magnitsky, Sergei 25 handwritten notes filed at Butyrka prison between July 26th 2008 and September 2009 post on the Untouchable websitehttp://russian-untouchables.com/docs/D107.pdf

41. Public Oversight Committee Report English translation (not the one given to PACER) http://online.wsj.com/public/resources/documents/WSJ-20091229-MagnitskyReport.pdf. Public Oversight Committee report as submitted to Wall Street Journal

42. Physicians' for Human Rights Report https://s3.amazonaws.com/PHR_Reports/magnitsky-report-july2011.pdf. Physician for Human Right report Cambridge MA.

43. Picture of altered phrase https://twitter.com/Justafool2764/status/1120403876425936896/photo/1. Picture of altered report from " special means were" to " a rubber baton was"

44. To be very clear, this is a different Kuznetsov then the one Browder is accusing of also being involved in the theft of the Russian treasury money and the murder of Magnitsky. The other Kuznetsov' first name is Artem

45. Komisar, Lucy https://twitter.com/LucyKomisar/status/1147921528555745280?s=20

Notes

46. Proposed Magnitsky List https://issuu.com/usa-s/docs/magnitsky List of submission of alleged candidates

47. Gremina, Elena Translation of play One HourEighteen Minutes

48. Browder, Bill. *Red Notice: How I Became Putin's No. 1 Enemy.* Simon and Schuster Books, 2016. (Page 276-277)

49. European Court of Human Rights report *1https://hudoc.echr.coe.int/eng?i=001-195527#{%22itemid%22:[%22001-195527%22]}*

50. "Browder and Kara Murza at University of Chicago 2019." YouTube, YouTube, *www.youtube.com/watch?v=Ux51Bqc3Un0.* (52)

51. Interesting trivia, Michael McFaul's debate partner on the debate question about repealing the Jackson -Vanik amendment was Steve Daines, now a Senator from Montana

52. McFaul, Michael. *From Cold War to Hot Peace: the inside Story of Russia and America.* Penguin Books, 2019. (54- pages 364-371)

53. "Podesta emails" https://wikileaks.org/podesta-emails/emailid/303. Hillary campaign day wrap up describing how they were able to "kill a story"

54. Lyn De Rothschild sued Henry Jackson Society for breach of trust claiming a program about Inclusive Capitalism was her idea.

55. Lyn De Rothschild wrote on Twitter to @Johnpodesta "this is pathetic; HRC lost because you ran an arrogant out of touch campaign: you have destroyed a great family and are a loser.

56. Brahm, Kristoffer and Jette Aagaard of Finans Danish Newspaper Questions and Answers with Bill Browder

57. Otto, Robert. Otto also has frequent exchanges with David Kramer, non resident fellow at the McCain Institute. See leaked

emails and search Kramer

58. Starova, Rimma https://www.thekomisarscoop.com/wp-content/uploads/2019/05/Starova-Testimony-10-July-08-1.pdf. Interrogation of the Victim April 2008. Rimma Starova

59. R/P/M is just an abbreviation for the 3 companies that were involved in the Russian treasury theft Rilend, Parfenion, and Makhaon. Also I place the word "End" at the end of the 3 paragraph excerpts from Starova testimony.

60. "Klyuev gang" John Wortley Hunt, Andrew Moray Stuart and Damian Calderba

61. Browder, Bill. Browder's answer to a Danish newspaper Finnan on why he ran from subpoenas

62. Simpson, Glenn R., and Peter Fritsch. Crime in Progress: inside the Steele Dossier and the Fusion GPS Investigation of Donald Trump. Random House, 2019.

63. Browder, Bill. Red Notice: How I Became Putin's No. 1 Enemy. Simon and Schuster Books, 2016.

64. Perepilichny poisoning Story by Jeffrey E. Stern. "An Enemy of the Kremlin Dies in London." *The Atlantic*, Atlantic Media Company, 3 Jan. 2017, www.theatlantic.com/magazine/archive/2017/01/the-poison-flower/508736/. (66)

65. Browder claims Navalny is the leader of the "Opposition" even though he polls at 2% and states "If there were free and fair elections in Russia, Navalny would be President and Putin would be in jail". The leader of the opposition party is Gennady Zyuganov whose Communist Party holds 43 seats in Duma.

66. Harding, Luke, and Shaun Walker. "'Poisoned' Russian Whistleblower Was Fatalistic over Death Threats."

The Guardian, Guardian News and Media, 19 May 2015, www.theguardian.com/uk-news/2015/may/19/poisoned-russian-whistleblower-was-fatalistic-over-death-threats.

67. Idib

68. Wright, Dan. "US State Media Merges With Right Wing Interpreter Mag." *Shadowproof*, 5 Jan. 2016, shadowproof.com/2016/01/05/us-state-media-merges-with-right-wing-interpreter-mag/. Article about Michael Weiss's Mag merging with RFE/RL (70)

69. Kasparov, Garry. I heard Garry say this when I attended the Oslo Freedom Forum in New York in 2018 Robert Otto's hacked emailhttps://en.news-front.info/2017/07/14/us-state-department-official-robert-otto-got-hacked/

70. Gasanov, Mikhail. Corporate Strategies in Post Communism Russia

71. Levy, Gordon Thor sued Fusion GPS for libel in their research on him. Fusion GPS lawyer, Levy, says Thor's lawsuit is a farce and a desperate attempt by Trump associates to distance themselves from Russia.

INDEX

RUSSIAN GOVERNMENT EMPLOYEES

Vladimir Putin
Dmitry Medvedev
Pavel Karpov
Artem Kuznetsov
Yury Chaika
Saak Kareptyan (deceased)

AMERICAN GOVERNMENT EMPLOYEES

Donald Trump
Barack Obama
Hillary Clinton
John Kerry
John McCain (deceased)
Joe Biden
Michael McFaul
Chuck Grassley
Ben Cardin

Kyle Parker
Robert Otto
Jonathan Winer
John Williams

TRUMP TOWER MEETING

Donald Trump Jr
Jared Kushner
Paul Manafort

Nataliya Veselnitskaya
Rinat Akhmetshin
Rob Goldstone
Irakly "Ike" Kaveladze
Anatoli Samachornov

PREVEZON VS U.S CASE

Baker Hostetler
Glenn Simpson Fusion GPS
Louis Freeh
Nataliya Veselnitskaya
Denis Katsyv
Prevezon Holdings Ltd

Bill Browder
Preet Bharara
Nickolai Gorokhov
John Ashcroft

HERMITAGE CAPITAL AND FIRESTONE DUNCAN EMPLOYEES

HERMITAGE
Bill Browder
Vadim Kleiner
Ivan Cherkasov
Eduard Khairetdinov
Paul Wrench
Martin Wilson
Kalymikia residents including Alexi Bokavev

FIRESTONE DUNCAN
Jamie Firestone
Sergei Magnitsky
Thomas Duncan (deceased)
Konstantin Ponomarev (ex-employee)
Victor Poryugin pseudonym for employee beat during the raid

"FAKE" HERMITAGE EMPLOYEES

Octai Gasanov (deceased)
Valery Kurochkin (deceased)

Vicktor Markelov
Victor Khlebnikov

Rimma Starova

Sergei Korobeinikov (deceased) Owner of Bank involved in theft

Index

Others accused and caught up in the scam

Alexander Perepilichny (deceased) Browder claims moved $6 million of the $38 million the Stepanovs are accused of stealing. Investor for two tax office employees accused of embezzling $38 million

Olga Stepanova and Vladen Stepanov. Accused of stealing $38 million
Olga Tzymai accused of helping with tax fraud in "Law and Order" video
Sergei Zhemchuzhnikov accused of helping with tax fraud in "Law and Order video"
Andrey Pavlov lawyer

REAL COMPANIES NAMES

Saturn Investment (Kalmykia)
Dalnaya Step (Kalmykia, Russia)

Kameya (Moscow)

Rilend. (Kalymykia, Russia)
Parfenion. (Moscow)
Makhaon. (Moscow)

Glendora Holdings (Cyprus)
Kone Holding (Cyprus)
HSBC Management Limited (Guernsey)

HSBC Private Bank (Guernsey)

"FAKE" COMPANIES

000 Rilend (Moscow)
000 Parfenion (Moscow)
000 Makhaon (Moscow)

000 Pluton (Kazan, Tatarstan)

Boily Systems (British Virgin Islands)

Logo Plus (St Petersburg)
Grand Aktive (Kazan)
Instar (Moscow)